OCR GCSE

Religious Studies A
World Religion(s)

Perspectives on Christian Ethics

Vicky Bunting · Janet Dyson
Gordon Kay · Ina Taylor · Cavan Wood

Series editor: Janet Dyson
Series consultant: Jon Mayled

www.heinemann.co.uk

✓ Free online support
✓ Useful weblinks
✓ 24 hour online ordering

01865 888080

Official Publisher Partnership

OCR AND HEINEMANN ARE WORKING TOGETHER TO PROVIDE BETTER SUPPORT FOR YOU

Heinemann is an imprint of Pearson Education Limited, a company incorporated in England and Wales, having its registered office at Edinburgh Gate, Harlow, Essex, CM20 2JE. Registered company number: 872828

www.heinemann.co.uk

Heinemann is a registered trademark of Pearson Education Limited Text © Pearson Education Limited 2009

First published 2009

British Library Cataloguing in Publication Data
A catalogue record for this book is available from the British Library

ISBN 978-0-435-50270-6

Edited by Bruce Nicholson
Reviewed by Reverend Paul Hedworth
Proofread by Tracey Smith
Project managed and typeset by Wearset Ltd, Boldon, Tyne and Wear
Original illustrations © Pearson Education Limited 2009
Illustrated by Wearset Ltd
Picture research by Q2AMedia
Cover photo/illustration © Shangara Singh/Alamy
Printed in Great Britain by Ashford Colour Press Ltd

Acknowledgements
The author and publisher would like to thank the following individuals and organisations for permission to reproduce photographs:
Page 2 Image Source/Jupiter Images. Page 4 Photofusion Picture Library/Alamy. Page 6 Pascal Genest/Istockphoto. Page 8 Chris Young/Associated Press. Page 11 Jason Burtt/Silverringthings. Page 16 Tom Stewart/Corbis. Page 18 Dr Najeeb Layyous/Science Photo Library. Page 21 Content Mine International/Alamy. Page 23 Caters News Agency Ltd/Rex Features. Page 30 Sanjay Rawat. Page 32 Mohsin Raza/Reuters. Page 35 ImageState/Alamy. Page 36 Rob Griffith/Associated Press. Page 38 Andresr/Shutterstock. Page 44 J-N. Reichel/Jupiter Images. Page 60 Nabil Al-Jurani/Associated Press. Page 62 Spanish School (10th century)/Church of San Isidoro, Leon, Spain/Giraudon/The Bridgeman Art Library. Page 66 Tom Grill/Corbis. Page 72 Nyul/Fotolia. Page 74 Hulton Archive/Getty Images. Page 76 Andy Myatt/Alamy. Page 77 Associated Press. Page 78 London Photos – Homer Sykes/Alamy. Page 80 Arcaid/Alamy.

The authors and publisher would like to thank the following for permission to use copyright material:
Bible scripture quotations taken from The Holy Bible, New International Version Anglicised Copyright © 1979, 1984 by International Bible Society. Used by permission of Hodder & Stoughton Publishers, a division of Hachette (UK) Ltd. All rights reserved. 'NIV' is a registered trademark of International Bible Society. UK trademark number 1448790.

Every effort has been made to contact copyright holders of material reproduced in this book. Any omissions will be rectified in subsequent printings if notice is given to the publishers.

Contents

Introduction

A note for teachers

This student book has been written especially to support the Christianity sections of OCR Religious Studies Specification A, Units B589: *Perspectives on World Religions* and B603: *Ethics 1*. It is part of an overall series for the OCR Specification A, which comprises:

- a series of Student Books covering Christianity, Christianity from a Roman Catholic Perspective, Islam, and Judaism – further details on pages viii and ix
- a series of Teacher Guides: one covering Christianity, Islam and Judaism, and another three covering Buddhism, Hinduism and Sikhism – further details on pages viii and ix.

Who are we?

The people who have planned and contributed to these books include teachers, advisers, inspectors, teacher trainers and GCSE examiners, all of whom have specialist knowledge of Religious Studies. For all of us the subject has a real fascination and we believe that good Religious Studies can make a major contribution to developing the skills, insights and understanding people need in today's world. In the initial development of this series, Pamela Draycott lent us her expertise, which we gratefully acknowledge.

Why is Religious Studies an important subject?

We believe that Religious Studies is an important subject because every area of life is touched by issues to do with religion and belief. Following a Religious Studies GCSE course will enable students to study and explore what people believe about God, authority, worship, beliefs, values and truth. Students will have opportunities to engage with questions about why people believe in God and how beliefs can influence many aspects of their lives.

Students will also explore why members of a particular religion may believe different things. In lessons students will be expected to think, talk, discuss, question and challenge, reflect on and assess a wide range of questions. As young people growing up in a diverse society, studying religion will help them to understand and relate to people whose beliefs, values and viewpoints differ from their own, and help them to deal with issues arising not only in school, but also in the community and workplace.

The study of religion will also help students to make connections with a whole range of other important areas, such as music, literature, art, politics, economics and social issues.

The specification for OCR A Perspectives on Christian Ethics

The specification outlines the aims and purposes of GCSE. The content to be covered is divided into six different Topics. The book's structure follows these Topic divisions precisely:

Topic 1: Religion and human relationships (Unit B603)

Topic 2: Religion and medical ethics (Unit B603)

Topic 3: Religion, poverty and wealth (Unit B603)

Topic 4: Responsibility for the planet (Unit B589)

Topic 5: War, peace and human rights (Unit B589)

Topic 6: Prejudice and equality (Unit B589)

The Topics focus on developing skills such as analysis, empathy and evaluation, which will enable students to gain knowledge and understanding of the specified content.

In following this specification students will have the opportunity to study Perspectives on Christian Ethics in depth and will learn about Christianity's diversity and the way in which people who believe it follow its teachings in their everyday lives.

This book covers everything students will need to know for the examination and shows them how to use their knowledge and understanding to answer the questions they will be asked.

Changes to the specification

The specification has changed dramatically according to the developing nature of education and the need for students to meet the demands of the world. The new specification will be taught from September 2009 onwards. The main changes that teachers and students should be aware of include the following:

- The Assessment Objectives (AOs) have changed, with a 50 per cent focus now given to AO1 (Describe, explain and analyse, using knowledge and understanding) and a 50 per cent focus to AO2 (Use evidence and reasoned argument to express and evaluate personal responses, informed insights and differing viewpoints). Previously, the balance was 75 per cent to 25 per cent respectively. There is more information on this on pages x and xi.

- There is an increased focus on learning *from* religion rather than simply learning *about* religion, and explicit reference to religious beliefs is now required in answers marked by Levels of Response.

- Levels of Response grids have been changed to a new range of 0 to 6 marks for AO1 questions and 0 to 12 marks for AO2 questions. The complete grids are reproduced on pages x and xi.

- Quality of Written Communication (QWC) is now only assessed on parts (d) and (e) of each question.

- Beyond the six Topics covered by this book, there is now a greater choice of Topics within the specification including a new Christian Scriptures paper on the Gospels of Mark and Luke, a paper on Muslim texts and a paper on Jewish texts.

- There is more freedom to study different combinations of religions and Topics.

Why did we want to write these resources?

We feel strongly that there is a need for good classroom resources that take advantage of the changed Assessment Objectives which:

- make the subject lively, interactive and relevant to today's world

- encourage students to talk to each other and work together

- challenge students and encourage them to think in depth in order to reach a high level of critical thinking

- train students to organise their thoughts in writing in a persuasive and structured way, and so prepare them for examination

The book has many features which contribute towards these goals. **Grade Studio** provides stimulating and realistic exercises to train students in what examiners are looking for and how to meet those expectations. **Exam Café** provides an exciting environment in which students can plan and carry out their revision.

Of course learning is about more than just exams. Throughout the book you will find **Research Notes**, which encourage students to explore beyond the book and beyond the curriculum. All of these features are explained in more detail on the next two pages.

What is in this book?

This student book has the following sections:

- the **Introduction**, which you are reading now
- the six **Topics** covered in the specification
- **Exam Café** – an invaluable resource for students studying their GCSE in Religious Studies
- **Glossary** – a reference tool for key terms and words used throughout the book.

Each of the above is covered in more detail in the text below.

The six Topics

Each Topic in this book contains:

- a Topic scene-setter, which looks at the key questions raised by the Topic, and the key words associated with those questions (**The Big Picture**)
- two-page spreads covering the **main Topic content**
- two pages of different level questions to check understanding of the Topic material (**Remember and Reflect**)
- exam-style questions with level indicators, examiner's comments and model answers (**Grade Studio**).

These features, which are explained more fully in the following pages, have been carefully planned and designed to draw together the OCR specification in an exciting but manageable way.

The Big Picture

This provides an overview of the Topic. It presents the requirements of the specification in a student friendly way. It includes a section, **Did you know?**, which offers a selection of thought-provoking, often surprising facts and observations from the Topic's contents, designed to engage and excite students about the content. This is followed by a useful reference list of **Key Words**. Finally, there is a **Get started** activity, often linked to a picture or visual stimulus, which presents a task also designed to engage students in the issues.

Main Topic content

The main content of each Topic is covered in a number of two-page spreads. Each spread equates to roughly one lesson of work – although teachers will need to judge for themselves if some of these need more time.

Each spread begins with the learning outcomes, highlighted in a box at the top of the page, so that students are aware of the focus and aims of the lesson. The text then attempts to answer, from a balanced viewpoint, one or two of the key questions raised in **Did you know?**. The text carefully covers the views of both religious believers and non-believers. It is also punctuated with activities that range from simple tasks that can take place in the classroom to more complex tasks that can be tackled away from school.

A range of margin features adds extra depth and support to the main text both for students and the teacher.

- **For debate** invites students to examine two sides of a controversial issue.
- **Must think about!** directs students towards a key idea that they should consider.
- **Sacred text** provides an extract from Christian sacred texts to help students understand religious ideas and teachings.
- **Research notes** provide stimulating ideas for further research beyond the material covered in the book and in the OCR specification.

Activities

Every Topic has a range of interesting activities which will help students to achieve the learning outcomes. Every two-page spread has a short starter activity to grab students' attention and to get them thinking. This is followed by a development section where the main content is introduced, and a plenary activity, which may ask students to reflect on what they have learnt, or may start them thinking about the next steps.

All activities are labelled **AO1** or **AO2** so you can tell at a glance which skills will be developed.

Remember and Reflect

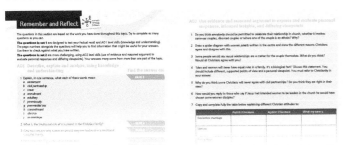

This provides an opportunity for students to reflect on what they have learned and identify possible weaknesses or gaps in their knowledge. It also helps them to recognise key ideas in the specification content. Once they have tested their knowledge with the first set of questions, a cross-reference takes them back to the relevant part of the text so they can check their answers. A second set of questions helps them to develop the AO2 skills necessary for the examination.

What is Grade Studio?

Everyone has different learning needs and this section of the book gives clear focus on how, with guidance from the teacher, students can develop the skills that will help them to achieve the higher levels in their exam responses.

Grade Studio appears as a two-page spread at the end of every Topic. It includes tips from the examiner, guidance on the steps to completing a well-structured answer, and sample answers with examiner comments.

What is the Exam Café?

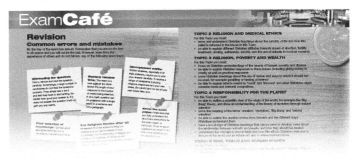

This is the revision section of the book. Here students will find useful revision tools and tips on how to get started on their revision and exam preparation. Students will also find assessment advice, including examples of different types of questions and samples of frequently asked questions. A useful **revision check list** allows students to review each Topic's content and explains where to find material in the book that relates to the exam questions.

Exam Café also has:

- sample student answers with examiner's comments
- help on understanding exam language, so students can achieve higher grades
- examiner tips, including common mistakes to be avoided.

Heinemann's OCR Religious Studies A Series

Below is a snapshot of the complete OCR Religious Studies A series. Further detail can be found at www.heinemann. co.uk/gcse

Note: Teachers using this Student Book will find the OCR B Philosophy and Applied Ethics Teacher Guide (ISBN 978-0-435-50152-5) useful when designing their course. The Teacher Guide gives full coverage of Unit B603: Ethics 1 (Relationships, Medical Ethics, Poverty and Wealth), which corresponds exactly to Topics 1–3 of this Student Book. In addition, the Teacher Guide covers Unit B604: Ethics 2. Much of this material will also be useful for Teachers when preparing Topics 4–6 of this Student Book for classroom teaching.

Christianity Student Book

ISBN 978-0-435-50130-3

This book provides complete coverage of both units of Christianity (B571 and B572). It provides information, activities, and Grade Studio examples for all aspects of the course, as well as an 8-page Exam Café for revision. Comprehensive support for the Teacher is provided through the corresponding OCR A Teacher Guide (see opposite).

Judaism Student Book

ISBN 978-0-435-50133-4

This book provides complete coverage of both units of Judaism (B579 and B580). It provides information, activities, and Grade Studio examples for all aspects of the course, as well as an 8-page Exam Café for revision. Comprehensive support for the Teacher is provided through the corresponding OCR A Teacher Guide (see below).

Islam Student Book

ISBN 978-0-435-50134-1

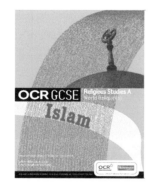

This book provides complete coverage of both units of Islam (B577 and B578). It provides information, activities, and Grade Studio examples for all aspects of the course, as well as an 8-page Exam Café for revision. Comprehensive support for the Teacher is provided through the corresponding OCR A Teacher Guide (see below).

OCR A Teacher Guide – Christianity, Islam and Judaism, with editable CD-ROM

ISBN 978-0-435-50136-5

This Teacher Guide covers Christianity, Islam and Judaism. It corresponds throughout to the Student Books and contains lesson plans, worksheets and Grade Studios to provide a complete teaching course for the chosen religion(s). The Christianity section of the Teacher Guide covers each Topic in the specification with six sample lesson plans and worksheets. The other religions have three sample lesson plans and worksheets. Everything is cross-referenced to the student books to help Teachers make the most out of these resources.

Finally, the Teacher Guide comes with an editable CD-ROM, which contains all the lesson plans along with fully customisable versions of all the worksheets.

Roman Catholic Student Book

ISBN 978-0-435-50132-7

This book provides complete coverage of both units of Christianity (Roman Catholic) (B573 and B574). It provides information, activities, and Grade Studio examples for all aspects of the course, as well as an 8-page Exam Café for revision.

OCR A Teacher Guide – Buddhism

ISBN 978-0-435-50129-7

This Teacher Guide covers Buddhism. It contains lesson plans, worksheets and Grade Studios to provide a complete teaching course for Buddhism. It covers Units B569 and B570 in the OCR A specification.

OCR A Teacher Guide – Hinduism

ISBN 978-0-435-50128-0

This Teacher Guide covers Hinduism. It contains lesson plans, worksheets and Grade Studios to provide a complete teaching course for Hinduism. It covers Units B575 and B576 in the OCR A specification.

OCR A Teacher Guide – Sikhism

ISBN 978-0-435-50127-3

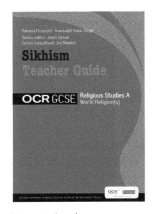

This Teacher Guide covers Sikhism. It contains lesson plans, worksheets and Grade Studios to provide a complete teaching course for Sikhism. It covers Units B581 and B582 in the OCR A specification.

Assessment Objectives and Levels of Response

Assessment Objectives, AO1 and AO2

In the new specification, the questions in the examination are designed to test students against two Assessment Objectives: AO1 and AO2. In the specification 50 per cent of the marks will be awarded for AO1 questions and 50 per cent will be awarded for AO2 questions.

AO1 Questions require candidates to 'describe, explain and analyse, using knowledge and understanding'.

AO2 Questions require candidates to 'use evidence and reasoned argument to express and evaluate personal responses, informed insights, and differing viewpoints'.

Each question in the examination is composed of 5 parts, a–e. In more detail:

- Parts **a–c** are worth one, two and three marks respectively and test a candidate's knowledge (AO1 skills).
- Part **d** is worth six marks and tests a candidate's understanding (AO1 skills).
- Part **e** is worth twelve marks and tests a candidate's AO2 skills.

LEVELS OF RESPONSE FOR MARKING AO1 PART (D) QUESTIONS

LEVEL 1

(1–2 marks)

A **weak** attempt to answer the question.

Candidates will demonstrate little understanding of the question.

- A small amount of relevant information may be included.
- Answers may be in the form of a list with little or no description/explanation/analysis.
- There will be little or no use of specialist terms.
- Answers may be ambiguous or disorganised.
- Errors of grammar, punctuation and spelling may be intrusive.

LEVEL 2

(3–4 marks)

A **satisfactory** answer to the question.

Candidates will demonstrate some understanding of the question.

- Information will be relevant but may lack specific detail.
- There will be some description/explanation/analysis although this may not be fully developed.
- The information will be presented for the most part in a structured format.
- Some use of specialist terms, although these may not always be used appropriately.
- There may be errors in spelling, grammar and punctuation.

LEVEL 3

(5–6 marks)

A **good** answer to the question.

Candidates will demonstrate a clear understanding of the question.

- A fairly complete and full description/explanation/analysis.
- A comprehensive account of the range and depth of relevant material.
- The information will be presented in a structured format.
- There will be significant, appropriate and correct use of specialist terms.
- There will be few, if any, errors in spelling, grammar and punctuation.

LEVELS OF RESPONSE FOR MARKING AO2 PART (E) QUESTIONS

LEVEL 0

(0 marks)

No evidence submitted or response does not address the question.

LEVEL 1

(1–3 marks)

A **weak** attempt to answer the question.

Candidates will demonstrate little understanding of the question.

- Answers may be simplistic with little or no relevant information.
- Viewpoints may not be supported or appropriate.
- Answers may be ambiguous or disorganised.
- There will be little or no use of specialist terms.
- Errors of grammar, punctuation and spelling may be intrusive.

LEVEL 2

(4–6 marks)

A **limited** answer to the question.

Candidates will demonstrate some understanding of the question.

- Some information will be relevant, although may lack specific detail.
- Only one view might be offered and developed.
- Viewpoints might be stated and supported with limited argument/discussion.
- The information will show some organisation.
- Reference to the religion studied may be vague.
- Some use of specialist terms, although these may not always be used appropriately.
- There may be errors in spelling, grammar and punctuation.

LEVEL 3

(7–9 marks)

A **competent** answer to the question.

Candidates will demonstrate a sound understanding of the question.

- Selection of relevant material with appropriate development.
- Evidence of appropriate personal response.
- Justified arguments/different points of view supported by some discussion.
- The information will be presented in a structured format.
- Some appropriate reference to the religion studied.
- Specialist terms will be used appropriately and for the most part correctly.
- There may be occasional errors in spelling, grammar and punctuation.

LEVEL 4

(10–12 marks)

A **good** answer to the question.

Candidates will demonstrate a clear understanding of the question.

- Answers will reflect the significance of the issue(s) raised.
- Clear evidence of an appropriate personal response, fully supported.
- A range of points of view supported by justified arguments/discussion.
- The information will be presented in a clear and organised way.
- Clear reference to the religion studied.
- Specialist terms will be used appropriately and correctly.
- Few, if any, errors in spelling, grammar and punctuation.

Topic 1: Religion and human relationships

The Big Picture

In this Topic, you will be addressing religious beliefs and teachings about:

- the roles of men and women in a Christian family
- marriage and marriage ceremonies
- divorce
- sexual relationships and contraception.

You will also think about the ways in which these beliefs affect the life and outlook of Christians in today's world.

DID YOU KNOW?

- Some Christians accept civil partnerships.
- Faithfulness and commitment are valued highly by Christians.
- Marriage takes place in church but a legal divorce can only take place in court.

KEY WORDS

adultery A married person having a sexual relationship with someone to whom they are not married.

annulment A marriage terminated by the Church because it was not valid.

civil partnership Legal recognition of a same-sex relationship with a registry office ceremony.

commitment A bond between a couple.

divorce The legal ending of a marriage.

pre-marital sex Having a sexual relationship before marriage.

promiscuity Having many sexual partners without commitment.

re-marriage Marrying again after divorce. Also after annulment or widowhood.

sacrament A special action which brings Christians closer to God.

vows Sacred promises a couple make at their marriage.

GET STARTED

In pairs, list ten qualities you think make a good relationship between a man and a woman.

For many Christians marriage is a sacrament.

Roles of men and women in a Christian family

The next two pages will help you to:

- explore the traditional roles of men and women in a Christian family
- identify the roles of men and women in the Church family
- evaluate the different roles of men and women.

AO1 skills **ACTIVITIES**

What are the roles of the man and the woman in a traditional Christian family?

Some Christian denominations allow women to become ministers.

Traditional roles in a Christian family

Some Christians interpret the second Genesis creation story, which says that God created Adam first, to mean that men are the superior sex. The story tells how Eve was created from Adam's rib bone in order to be his helper. Because Eve was the one who led Adam astray in the Garden of Eden, some Christians believe this teaches that women are the weaker sex.

Some Christians who hold traditional views on marriage believe that the man is the head of a Christian family. In a Christian marriage ceremony the bride would make a vow to obey her husband. Christian women look to Mary, the mother of Jesus, as the role model of a quiet, loving mother. It is the wife's duty to provide a loving home for her husband and children.

They may regard the man as the head of the family with the duty to provide for his wife and children by earning the money. Within the house he sets the rules and leads his family by setting a good example of how a Christian should behave.

These roles are supported by scriptures. St Paul, in his letters to the early Church, gave clear directions that women were to obey their husbands because God had created them that way.

Ephesians 5:22–23a
Wives, submit to your husbands as to the Lord. For the husband is the head of the wife as Christ is the head of the Church.

An alternative view of roles in the Christian family

Most modern Christians do not believe that men are superior to women. They accept that men and women are different, but believe the Bible is saying both are equal in the eyes of God. This is because in the first creation story it simply says God created human beings to be like himself and that 'male and female he created them' (Genesis 1:27b).

These views are supported with other passages in the New Testament such as:

> **Galatians 3:28**
>
> *'There is neither… male or female… for you are all one in Christ Jesus.'*

Most Christians in today's society believe in an equal relationship where the roles of the couple are interchangeable. Some women work to provide for the family and some men share child-care and household duties.

Traditional roles within the Church family

Many Christians think of the members of their religion as one big family, where everyone has a distinct role to play; they call this the Church family. Following Old Testament passages about the superiority of men, St Paul taught that women should be silent in church.

Christians suggest that because Jesus chose 12 men to be his disciples, he clearly intended men to take the leading role in the Church. From the disciples Jesus chose Peter to lead the Church and, according to tradition, it was Peter who became the Bishop of Rome, the first Pope. Roman Catholics believe Jesus intended men to be leaders of the Church family and every Pope who has followed Peter has been male. Indeed Roman Catholics do not permit women to become priests.

Other views of the role of men and women in the Church family

Liberal Protestants look at Jesus' treatment of women for guidance. Even though he lived at a time when women had few rights in society, Jesus permitted them to be his followers and showed them respect.

The story of Martha and Mary (Luke 10:38–42) shows Jesus encouraging a woman to sit at his feet in order to learn from him. This was not something women were usually allowed to do.

Christians believe that because the risen Christ chose to reveal himself to women first on Easter morning that it was clear that he held women in high regard.

All this leads less traditional Christians to believe men and women can have an equal role in Church leadership. Most non-conformist Churches permit women to be ministers and the Anglican Church ordained its first women priests in 1994.

> **1 Corinthians 11b–12a**
>
> *'… woman is not independent of man, nor is man independent of woman. For as woman came from man, so also man is born of woman.'*

> **1 Timothy 2:11–13**
>
> *A woman should learn in quietness and full submission. I do not permit a woman to teach or have authority over a man; she must be silent. For Adam was formed first, then Eve.*

AO2 skills ACTIVITIES

Write an article for a parish magazine explaining why that particular church believes it is wrong to have a woman priest. Then write a 'letter to the editor' from a female vicar giving the reasons why she thinks that church is wrong.

Marriage and marriage ceremonies

The next two pages will help you to:

- examine marriage ceremonies
- explore how ceremonies reflect Christian teaching about marriage
- evaluate responses to civil partnerships.

Marriage ceremonies

Marriage is both a civil and a religious **commitment** for Christians. The Christian **marriage** is a civil ceremony because the couple's relationship is publicly witnessed by the congregation and the marriage register is signed. Christians also believe that marriage is a holy relationship. It is also seen by many Christians as a **sacrament** and part of God's plan for humanity. Through marriage a couple can enjoy a loving relationship with each other that enables God to channel his love for them. Because Christian marriage is a religious commitment, the ceremony takes place in a church or a chapel.

This is how the Catholic Church describes marriage:

66 *Marriage is the sacrament in which baptized men and women vow to belong to each other in a permanent and exclusive sexual partnership of loving, mutual care, concern and shared responsibility, in the hope of having children and bringing up a family.* 99   (Catholic Truth Society)

All Christians believe the purpose of marriage is to:

- help and support each other in good and bad times
- enjoy a sexual relationship
- have children and bring them up in a Christian family.

At a Christian marriage, the ring symbolises that the marriage will be forever.

What happens in a Christian marriage ceremony?

Although many church weddings are quite lavish affairs, the Christian marriage ceremony is very simple. It requires only the couple, a priest, a ring and two people to witness the ceremony in a church.

The couple will make a promise to each other in the marriage ceremony. It is called a vow because the promise is made in front of God.

66 *I_____, take you _____, to have and to hold, from this day forward: for better, for worse, for richer, for poorer, in sickness and in health, to love and to cherish, till death us do part, according to God's holy law, in the presence of God I make this vow.* 99

ACTIVITIES

Make a poster showing the main features of a Christian wedding and their meaning.

How does the marriage ceremony reflect Christian teachings?

Each part of the marriage ceremony has a meaning which is closely linked to Christian teachings about marriage and family life:

- The ceremony takes place in a church because promises are made in front of God.
- The priest asks the couple and the congregation if there are any reasons why this marriage cannot go ahead. This is to show that the Christian marriage is legally binding.
- The priest asks both the bride and the groom if they want to marry the other person. This is to show that Christian marriage is a relationship, that is entered into freely and no one has forced them to marry.
- Having children and bringing them up in the Christian faith is an important part of marriage and the priest explains this to couples in the opening address.
- Couples say their **vows** in the presence of God and the congregation of Christians as witnesses, showing the sacred importance of the ceremony.
- Prayers, Bible readings and the priest's talk teach the couple about the importance of love in a marriage.
- A ring is given to symbolise the unending nature of love and of Christian marriage. This shows a marriage is for life.

As part of the marriage ceremony, the priest asks the bride and groom 'Will you accept children lovingly from God, and bring them up according to the law of Christ and his Church?'

What do Christians think about civil partnerships?

Christianity teaches that sexual relationships only belong within marriage. For that reason, many Christians do not accept **civil partnerships**. There are several passages in the Bible that condemn same-sex relationships.

> **1 Corinthians 6:9**
>
> *Do you not know that the wicked will not inherit the kingdom of God? Neither the sexually immoral... nor homosexual offenders.*

The Catholic Church does not accept civil partnerships because it rejects same-sex relationships. In 2008 a Vatican official stated that 'Homosexuality is a disordered behaviour. The activity must be condemned', and the Pope told Catholics that homosexuality was a greater problem for the future of the world than climate change.

Some Christians accept civil partnerships as another form of loving relationship and permit same-sex couples to have a blessing ceremony after their civil partnership registration if they wish. Members of the Church of England vary in their response. Some priests will hold a blessing ceremony after a civil partnership and others will not.

 **RESEARCH NOTE**

Use the BBC news website to research the 2008 case of Lillian Ladele. What reasons did she give for her stand? What did the court decide? Who do you think was right?

 **ACTIVITIES**

Explain why some Christians might say a civil partnership cannot be regarded as a Christian marriage no matter how religious the couple are. What might the couple say?

Divorce

Christian beliefs about the ethics of divorce

Christian teachings and the marriage ceremony, both show Christians that marriage is intended to be a relationship for life. Marriage is a **holy relationship** and the **vows** a couple make are made in front of God and should never be broken. The ring given in the marriage ceremony symbolises that love is unending and that Jesus taught that marriage is for life. These beliefs mean there is much debate within Christianity about whether it is right or wrong to permit married couples to **divorce**.

Roman Catholic beliefs about the ethics of divorce

The reasons discussed above lead Roman Catholics and some Protestants to believe that divorce is wrong. They understand that not all marriages succeed and the Church will give a couple all the assistance it can to help them resolve their differences. When that fails the Catholic Church permits a couple to separate and live apart. It does not allow either of them to re-marry or to have a sexual relationship with anyone else because that would be **adultery**.

In exceptional cases the Catholic Church can officially annul a marriage. This declares that the marriage was not a true marriage and it is cancelled. The situation is the same as if the wedding had never taken place. An **annulment** can be granted if one of the couple was under-age, forced to marry against their will or unaware of what they were doing due to diminished responsibility. An annulment can also be granted if a marriage is not consummated (the couple do not have a sexual relationship after marriage).

The Catholic Catechism says '...men and women... in matrimony give themselves with a love that is total and therefore unique and exclusive' (§2387).

The next two pages will help you to:

- compare beliefs about the ethics of divorce
- examine Christian beliefs about the ethics of re-marriage
- evaluate Christian attitudes towards divorce.

HRH Prince Charles and Camilla Parker-Bowles could only have a blessing in church after their marriage because they had both been divorced.

AO1 skills ACTIVITIES

Why was the re-marriage of Prince Charles, heir to the throne and future head of the Church of England, such a difficult issue for the Church of England? The BBC news website may give you some additional information.

Church of England beliefs about the ethics of divorce

Although the Church of England and most Non-conformist Churches believe that marriage is for life, they accept things may not always work out. If this happens the priest will help a couple try to resolve their difficulties. If they are unable to, the Church of England accepts that divorce may be the kindest thing for all concerned because it ends conflict and enables the couple to begin a new life.

- Divorce is permitted because Jesus taught that the right course of action is the most loving thing to do. Forcing a couple to remain trapped in a loveless marriage would hurt them and everyone in their family, which cannot be right.
- Some Christians believe a marriage ends when love dies between the couple, as well as with the death of a partner.
- Others point out that Jesus did allow divorce for unfaithfulness.
- Jesus lived in a Jewish society almost 2000 years ago, so some Christians believe it is right to interpret his message in the light of today's society and permit divorce.

Only the Orthodox Church will grant a religious divorce. Otherwise it is a civil matter that is dealt with through the courts. The 1996 Family Law Act permits divorce for the irretrievable breakdown of a marriage which may have occurred because of adultery, unreasonable behaviour, desertion, two years' separation with consent or five years' separation without consent.

> ### Mark 10:10–11
> *Therefore what God has joined together, let no man separate. Anyone who divorces his wife and marries another woman commits adultery against her.*

> ### Matthew 5:32
> *But I tell you that anyone who divorces his wife, except for marital unfaithfulness, causes her to become an adulteress, and anyone who marries the divorced woman commits adultery.*

Christian beliefs about the ethics of re-marriage

Some Christians, such as Roman Catholics, do not accept re-marriage in church after a civil divorce. Other Christians accept **re-marriage** because Jesus also taught the importance of forgiveness if someone has made a mistake. However, not all Christians permit a second marriage ceremony to take place in church because the divorced partner would be making promises in front of God which they have already broken once.

The Church of England will accept either re-marriage in church, or a church blessing following a register office ceremony such as the Prince of Wales had. Because some vicars do not believe it is right to make promises which have been broken once, the Church allows them to refuse to carry out a re-marriage ceremony. The couple must marry in another church or with another priest.

 **AO2** skills **ACTIVITIES**

'My husband and I constantly argue about money. I think we should get divorced but Tim doesn't want to because we have a two-year-old we both love dearly. We are Christians and married in church but I think it's time for each of us to start a fresh life. What should we do?' Write a reply to this magazine letter giving your advice and reasons.

Sexual relationships and contraception

Beliefs about sexual relationships

Christians believe that sex is a gift from God to be enjoyed by a couple as an act of love within their marriage and in order to have children. Because sex is a relationship that has been blessed by God, Christians believe that casual sexual encounters are wrong.

There are many passages in the Bible which teach that sex outside marriage is forbidden. The seventh of the Ten Commandments forbids **adultery**, and some Christians interpret this as meaning that all sexual activity outside marriage is wrong.

Jesus also condemned adultery in the gospels (Mark 10:7–9). This leads some Christians, such as Roman Catholics and Evangelical Protestants, to reject all sexual relationships outside marriage. They believe a person should remain a virgin until they are married and have no other sexual partner during their marriage.

The Catechism of the Catholic Church is very clear about sexual relations: 'The sexual act must take place exclusively within marriage. Outside of marriage it always constitutes a grave sin' (CCC: §2390).

All Christians prefer sexual relationships to take place within a marriage because it provides a stable environment for bringing up children. However, some Christians are prepared to accept pre-marital sex as part of a loving relationship if a couple are committed to each other and plan to marry. This is because Jesus taught that love was what mattered most.

Differing views

Jesus' message of love leads some liberal Christians, such as Quakers, to accept that couples may choose to cohabit (live together without being married) and that some people may choose to enjoy same-sex relationships. These Christians argue that what matters most is the quality of a relationship.

The Church of England, and other Christian groups, believe that marriage is the correct place for a sexual relationship because the family is the best environment to bring up children. They do, however, accept that in today's society many people choose to cohabit as a prelude to getting married. For these reasons **pre-marital sex** may be accepted if marriage is to follow.

The next two pages will help you to:

- examine Christian beliefs about sexual relationships and contraception
- evaluate views about sexual relationships and contraception.

ACTIVITIES

Design an A5 flyer the Catholic Church could give teenagers attending one of their youth clubs, explaining Catholic views about sexual relationships outside marriage.

Adultery is something no Christian would accept because it involves deceit and causes suffering, which can never be right. Not only is it condemned in the Ten Commandments but it breaks the marriage **vows**. Fidelity and commitment are very important aspects of Christian teaching.

> **1 Corinthians 6:18–19a, 20b**
>
> *Flee from sexual immorality. All other sins a man commits are outside his body, but he who sins sexually sins against his own body. Do you not know that your body is a temple of the Holy Spirit … Therefore honour God with your body.*

Beliefs about contraception

Because the marriage ceremony states sex is given to a couple by God so they can have children, Roman Catholics reject the idea of artificial birth control. They believe that the act of sex should always be open to God's gift of a baby. This means the pill, condoms and all other contraceptive devices are forbidden. If a Catholic couple plan a family they are permitted to use a natural method of birth control such as the rhythm method.

Whilst all Christians believe that having children is an important part of marriage, some accept that couples may want to limit the size of their family. This could be for financial reasons or to make sure a woman's health does not suffer as a result of many pregnancies. Provided both husband and wife agree, most forms of contraception are acceptable. This frees a couple to enjoy a sexual relationship without the worry of an unwanted pregnancy. Using contraception to plan the timing of a pregnancy can help ensure that all children in the family are wanted, loved and provided for.

Because the marriage ceremony states that the purpose of marriage is to have children, most Christians do not approve of using contraception to prevent a couple from ever having a baby. For this reason, some Christians do not approve of sterilisation except for medical reasons.

Members of the Christian organisation the Silver Ring Thing promise to abstain from sex before marriage.

 **FOR DEBATE**

'Religion is about spirituality not sexuality.' Should Christians have rules about personal relationships? What do you think?

 **AO2** skills **ACTIVITIES**

Explain why some Christians accept contraception and others do not. Summarise Christian beliefs and attitudes about sexual relationships explaining different viewpoints.

Remember and Reflect

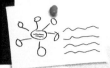

The questions in this section are based on the work you have done throughout this topic. Try to complete as many questions as you can.

The questions in set 1 are designed to test your factual recall and AO1 level skills (knowledge and understanding). The page numbers alongside the questions will help you to find information that might be useful for your answers. Use them to check against what you have written.

The questions in set 2 are more challenging, using AO2 level skills (use of evidence and reasoned argument to evaluate personal responses and differing viewpoints). Your answers many come from more than one part of the topic.

AO1 Describe, explain and analyse, using knowledge and understanding

Find the answer on:

1 Explain, in one sentence, what each of these words mean:
   a sacrament
   b civil partnership
   c vows
   d annulment
   e adultery
   f promiscuity
   g pre-marital sex
   h commitment
   i divorce
   j re-marriage
PAGE 2

2 What is the traditional role of a husband in the Christian family? **PAGE 4**

3 Give two reasons why a woman should obey her husband in a traditional Christian family. **PAGE 4**

4 What does the ring symbolise in a marriage? **PAGE 7**

5 Give two reasons why some Christians do not agree with divorce. **PAGE 8–9**

6 Explain why some Christians accept the use of contraception. **PAGE 11**

7 State two reasons why some Christians do not agree with sex before marriage. **PAGE 10**

8 Describe the Christian wedding ceremony. **PAGE 6–7**

9 What are the three purposes of marriage? **PAGE 6**

10 Explain why some Christians accept civil partnerships and others do not. **PAGE 7**

11 How is an annulment different from a divorce? **PAGE 8**

12 What is the Christian attitude to re-marriage? **PAGE 9**

13 Why do some Christians disagree with the use of contraception? **PAGE 11**

14 Explain why some Christians believe that men and not women should be Church leaders. **PAGE 5**

15 Explain the different Christian attitudes to sex outside marriage. **PAGE 10–11**

AO2 Use evidence and reasoned argument to express and evaluate personal responses, informed insights, and differing viewpoints

1 Do you think everybody should be permitted to celebrate their relationship in church, whether it involves same-sex couples, divorced couples or where one of the couple is an atheist? Why?

2 Draw a spider diagram with *women priests* written in the centre and show the different reasons Christians agree and disagree with this.

3 Some people would say sexual relationships are a matter for the couple themselves. What do you think? Would all Christians agree with you?

4 'Men and women will never have equal roles in a family. It's a biological fact!' Discuss this statement. You should include different, supported points of view and a personal viewpoint. You must refer to Christianity in your answer.

5 Why do you think some Christians will never agree with civil partnerships? Do you think they are right in their view?

6 How would you reply to those who say if Jesus had intended women to be leaders in the church he would have chosen some women disciples?

7 Copy and complete fully the table below explaining different Christian attitudes to:

	Permit it because	Against it because	What my view is
Sex before marriage			
Divorce			
Re-marriage			
Contraception			
Civil partnership			

GradeStudio

Welcome to the Grade Studio

Grade Studio is here to help you improve your grades by working through typical questions you might find on an examination paper. You will see different answers to the questions, showing you how you can improve each answer to get a better grade. There is not sufficient space in this book to give full answers so these answers offer you the skeleton structure of a response. In the exam you must answer as fully as you can.

How the grades work

OCR questions in Spec B always consist of five parts, **a–e**. Parts **a–c** test factual recall only (AO1). Part **d** is always a six-mark question testing understanding (AO1), and part **e** is always a 12-mark question testing evaluation and other AO2 skills.

For parts **a–c**, you need to revise the material for the Topic and make sure that you know it thoroughly – Grade Studio cannot help you with this!

However, for parts **d** and **e** you need to structure your answers to show your skills – and this is where you can use the Grade Studio to help you improve your answers.

Examiners use levels to measure the responses (these are marked in the answers below). You can find the actual levels that examiners will use to mark your answers on pages x–xi.

Graded examples for this topic

AO1

Assessment Objective one (AO1) requires you to 'describe, explain and analyse, using knowledge and understanding'. Here is an example of an AO1 question, along with a student's answers and an examiner's comments on those answers.

Question

How might a Christian marriage ceremony reflect belief?   **[6 marks]**

Student's answer

A Christian wedding ceremony reflects belief because the bride wears white, which represents chastity.

People also make vows to each other to say that they will always stay together and look after each other. If someone broke these vows, they might get divorced which is breaking the promise made before God in church.

Examiner's comment

The candidate has given a satisfactory answer to the question. There are two relevant points but only one of them, the vows, has any explanation. The answer does not really explain how the service reflects belief, it just states something true about the ceremony. The answer needs to give more information and examples in order to reach Level 3. The candidate could also use more technical terms from the specification to show the breadth of their knowledge and understanding.

Assessment Objective two (AO2) requires you to 'use evidence and reasoned argument to express and evaluate personal responses, informed insights, and differing viewpoints'. Here is an example of an AO2 question, along with a student's answers and an examiner's comments on those answers.

Question

'Divorce is wrong.' Discuss this statement. You should include different, supported points of view and a personal viewpoint. You must refer to Christianity in your answer. [12 marks]

Student's answer

Divorce is always wrong for Christians because they promise to stay together until 'death do us part'.
Some Christians might also say that if people do get divorced, they are breaking a promise they made to God when they married before a priest as well as to each other. This makes splitting up a really serious matter for Christians and because of this, many of them think divorce is always wrong.

Examiner's comment

The candidate has given a limited answer to the question. There are two relevant points but they both address the same issue and neither is expanded very far. In order to reach Level 4, the candidate needs to give alternative viewpoints and to include a personal response.

Student's improved answer

Divorce is always wrong for Christians because they promise to stay together until 'death do us part'.

Some Christians might also say that if people do get divorced, they are breaking a promise they made to God when they married before a priest as well as to each other. This makes splitting up a really serious matter for Christians and because of this, many of them think divorce is always wrong.

Examiner's comment

This is now a good answer to the question. The candidate has shown a clear understanding of the question and has presented a range of views supported by evidence and argument. The answer explains Christian views, amongst others, and includes a personal viewpoint, which is also supported.

On the other hand, some Christians may believe that, if a husband and wife are very unhappy together, they should consider a divorce rather than staying together and being miserable. This can also possibly have a bad effect on their children. Christians will always try to help a couple to stay together, but there are circumstances in which this is not possible. The evidence from the Bible is not clear because Jesus seemed to agree with divorce in the case of adultery. Also a key idea in Christianity is forgivness and some Christians believe divorced people, need to be forgiven so they can move on into a new relationship rather than be miserable for ever. I think divorce should be allowed.

My personal opinion is that sometimes people are just not suited to one another and that they are better off getting a divorce and having the opportunity to start their life again. However, I do think that it is important that the needs of any children are taken into account when a divorce takes place.

These specimen answers provide an outline of how you could construct your response. Space does not allow us to give a full response. The examiner will be looking for more detail in your actual exam responses.

Topic 2: Religion and medical ethics

The Big Picture

In this Topic you will be addressing Christian beliefs about:

- abortion and the reasons for different attitudes to this issue
- fertility treatment and attitudes to issues raised by fertility treatment and cloning
- euthanasia and suicide and the reasons for different attitudes to these issues
- the use of animals in medical research.

You will also think about your own feelings and responses to these questions and issues.

DID YOU KNOW?

- Every year at least 200,000 women have abortions in the UK.
- Some Christians believe abortion is the greatest moral evil.
- When anaesthetics were discovered in the nineteenth century some Christians accused doctors of 'playing God'.
- It is theoretically possible to choose the sex of a baby, perhaps for the reason of preventing the transmission of diseases which are carried by one gender; for example, muscular dystrophy affects only boys.

KEY WORDS

abortion Deliberate termination of pregnancy by removal and destruction of the foetus.

clone An individual organism or cell produced asexually from one ancestor to which they are genetically identical.

embryo A foetus before it is 4 months old.

euthanasia When someone is helped to die without pain before they would have died naturally.

fertility treatment Medical treatment to help a woman become pregnant.

genetic engineering The deliberate modification of the characteristics of an organism by manipulating its genetic material.

medical ethics Questions of morality that are raised by medical situations.

sacred/sanctity Holy, having something of God or the divine.

sanctity of life The belief that all life is given by God and is therefore sacred.

suicide Deliberately ending one's own life.

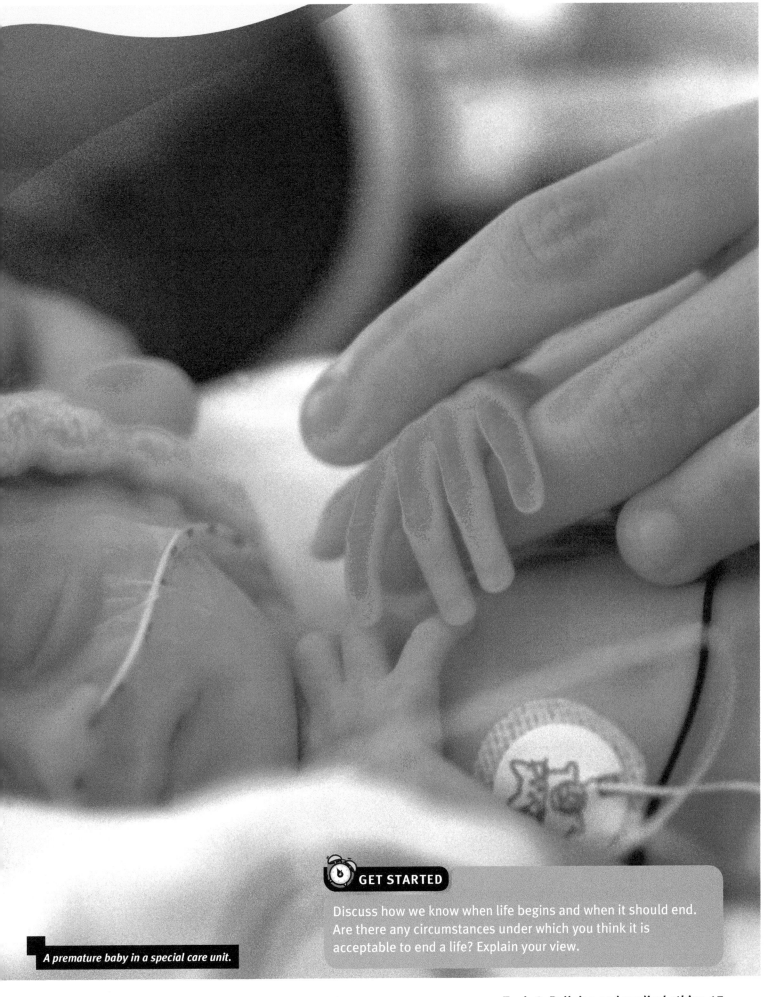

A premature baby in a special care unit.

GET STARTED

Discuss how we know when life begins and when it should end. Are there any circumstances under which you think it is acceptable to end a life? Explain your view.

Attitudes to abortion

What is medical ethics?

Medical ethics is about applying moral values to medical situations. The following questions are examples of the kind of dilemmas which medical ethics deals with:

- Should everyone have the right to have a child, helped by doctors if necessary?
- Should people be kept alive if they are very disabled or in great pain?
- Should women be able to end a pregnancy if they choose?

Is life sacred?

Many Christians have strong views about medical ethics because they believe that life is created by God. It is therefore **sacred** or holy and humans do not have the right to take it away. This is often described as the '**sanctity of life**' and is a concept used in arguments about whether particular actions are right or wrong. Knowing when a human life begins is very important for Christians in helping them to decide if and when abortion is acceptable.

When does human life begin?

Today many pregnant women have their first ultrasound scan at 8 weeks and are able to see, even at such an early stage, that their baby is beginning to be recognisably human.

Some doctors say that, although the technology used to produce pictures like this is fantastic, such images confuse people. Donald Peebles, a scientist at University College Hospital, London said in a newspaper interview that although the foetus clearly looks human by 12 weeks, proper sensory development takes place much later. He believed that there was risk that the pictures would make people assume that foetuses have more advanced brains than is the case. (*The Times*, 3 October 2006).

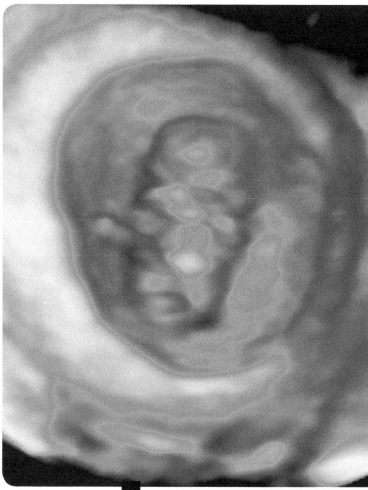

A 3D scan of a four-week-old foetus.

AO1 skills **ACTIVITIES**

With a partner write a sentence of not more than ten words explaining the meaning of the term 'sanctity of life'. Compare your sentence with others in the group.

What is abortion?

Abortion is the deliberate termination of pregnancy by the removal and destruction of the foetus. Each year in the UK more than 200,000 women have abortions. Around 4000 of those are on girls aged under 16, the legal age of consent for sex. In the UK abortions are legal if the foetus is less than 24 weeks old, provided two doctors consent to the abortion. It has to be done before the baby could live outside the womb without medical help.

Abortions over 24 weeks are only allowed in exceptional circumstances, for example, if there is a substantial risk that the child would be born with a serious disability, if the mother's life is in danger or if a woman has become pregnant as a result of rape.

Why do Christians disagree about abortion?

There is no specific teaching in the Bible about abortion so Christians have to apply their understanding of Christian principles to the situation. Different ways of interpreting the teachings in the Bible result in Christians having different attitudes to abortion.

Many Christians believe that all babies have a soul from the moment of conception and so are fully human. This is based on the teaching in Genesis 1:27 that people are made in the image of God; that God has a plan for every individual (Jeremiah 1:5) and that God is the creative spark from the moment of conception (Psalm 139:13). This means that they believe the foetus is fully human and therefore abortion is the same as murder.

Both the Church of England and the Roman Catholic Church teach that abortion is a great moral evil and that human life must be protected and respected from the moment of conception.

The Roman Catholic Church does not permit abortion under any circumstances unless it is the unintended but foreseeable result of an action, i.e. 'doctrine of double effect'. For example, when an operation necessary to save the life of the mother causes the abortion, such as in an ectopic pregnancy.

The Church of England teaches that abortion is only acceptable in exceptional circumstances, for example, if it is necessary to save the mother's life, if the pregnancy is the result of rape, or if the baby is likely to be severely disabled. Other Christians take a broader view but believe abortion should be a last resort, and the parents must make the final decision.

Genesis 1:27

So God created man in his own image, in the image of God he created him; male and female he created them.

Jeremiah 1:5a

Before I formed you in the womb I knew you, before you were born I set you apart.

RESEARCH NOTE

At 4–6 weeks the foetus is the size of a poppy seed; its heart is a single tube with a few uncoordinated beats; bones begin to form. Find out about the development of a foetus/embryo at 8, 12, 20, 28 and 40 weeks. How can this information be used in the arguments for and against abortion?

AO2 skills ACTIVITIES

'One question about all this is: why is it when I wanted the baby it was a baby, and when I didn't it was something else?' (Ellie, aged 20, in online chat room about abortion). How would you respond to Ellie's question? Explain your reasons.

What do Christians believe about fertility treatment?

The ethics of fertility treatment

Fertility treatment, cloning and **genetic engineering** raise some important ethical questions for many Christians. Three important beliefs affect the way Christians view these issues:

- God alone should be the creator of life.
- God gave humans a soul.
- God created humans in his image.

What is fertility treatment?

Fertility treatment is medical treatment given to help people who want babies but cannot have them. The reasons for infertility can be that the man is not producing healthy sperm or the woman is not producing eggs. Whatever the reason, infertility can make people very unhappy.

Christian responses to issues raised by fertility treatment

Christians do not agree about fertility treatment. Roman Catholics disagree with fertility treatment and teach that infertility must be accepted as part of God's plan. Many Christians think that medical help should be given to people who want babies. Some Christians think it is wrong to use sperm or eggs from a donor because it brings a third person into the marriage relationship.

In vitro fertilisation (IVF)

One of the most common fertility treatments is IVF, which stands for *In vitro* fertilisation – literally meaning 'in glass'. Doctors put healthy sperm and a human egg together in a test tube and wait to see if embryos develop. Embryos are then placed inside a woman's uterus where they can continue to grow. To ensure that at least one embryo survives doctors fertilise more than one egg. This process may result in spare embryos. Many Christians and non-religious people are concerned about what happens to these spare embryos.

Using donor sperm or eggs

Sometimes one partner cannot produce healthy sperm or eggs at all and donor sperm or eggs may be used. There are questions about whether it is acceptable to use donor sperm or eggs from someone who is unknown to the couple. Some Christians think this goes against the belief that partners should be faithful to each other.

The next two pages will help you to:

- explain and evaluate Christian responses to issues raised by fertility treatment and cloning
- reflect on your own views about these issues.

ACTIVITIES

With a partner think of as many reasons as you can why people might want to have children.

ACTIVITIES

Do spare embryos count as potential humans and would it be committing murder to throw them away if they are not needed?

Is it right to use embryos for medical research?

Christians believe in the **sanctity of life**. They believe life is a gift from God and trust that God has a purpose for each human life. The ability of scientists to use human embryos to **clone** human cells raises significant ethical problems for many Christians. Some Christians who are opposed to human cloning see it as morally equivalent to 'playing God'.

In embryo research human embryos are studied and used in order to find ways of preventing and curing illnesses. Human tissue from the embryos can be implanted into living patients to slow down serious diseases of the nervous system such as motor neurone disease and Parkinson's disease. This tissue usually comes from aborted foetuses.

Roman Catholics oppose all embryo research. Anglicans support it up to 14 days. Most Christians accept controlled embryo research. Some Christians think that embryo research is acceptable because it means that some good comes out of **abortions**. Others disagree because they think it is treating human life as a means to an end rather than as intrinsically valuable, and because the embryo is not in a position to give consent.

Is cloning playing God?

In 1996 the world's first cloned animal, Dolly the sheep, was created by cell fusion in which the nucleus of an already differentiated adult cell was fused with an unfertilised egg from a donor animal. It is theoretically possible to use this process to produce a child that is a clone, an exact image, of one of its parents.

Playing God: Frankenstein's Monster

In 1818 Mary Shelley's book *Frankenstein* was published. This tells the story of scientist Victor Frankenstein and the monster he created from parts of dead bodies with disastrous consequences. It seemed a total fantasy when it was written but, 200 years later, at the start of the 21st century, it no longer seems impossible.

Are we 'Playing God' by choosing the kind of baby we want?

She may never get breast cancer – but girl's birth raises new doubts over designer babies

In 2009 scientists announced that they had screened embryos for the purpose of reducing a baby's chance of getting breast cancer when she grows up. This was not a case of a so called 'designer baby' – her parents did not choose her hair colour or select an aptitude for maths or ice skating. They did it to ensure that she did not develop a life threatening disease and that she would not pass on the defective gene to her own children.

RESEARCH NOTE

'Religion should not interfere with how people conceive.'

Research on the Internet arguments for and against this statement.

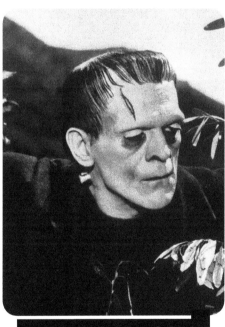

Frankenstein's monster as depicted in the film Frankenstein *(1931).*

AO2 skills ACTIVITIES

What arguments could be put forward to support the claim that a person created by cloning was 'made in the image of God'? Do you agree?

Attitudes to euthanasia and suicide

The next two pages will help you to:

- explain and evaluate Christian beliefs about euthanasia
- explain and evaluate Christian responses to suicide
- reflect on your own views about these issues.

Should we have the right to choose when we die?

Most Christians believe that God gives life and only God can decide when a life should be ended. Some Christians believe that as humans have free will they have a choice between life and death but to choose death, either by **euthanasia** or **suicide**, would be a sin.

AO1 skills ACTIVITIES

Discuss with a partner how you might support a friend who was feeling very depressed.

> **Job 1:21b**
> *The Lord gave and the Lord has taken away, may the name of the Lord be praised.*

Euthanasia, sometimes called 'mercy killing', means 'good or gentle death' and is used to describe situations where death is deliberately chosen either by the person or by people close to them if they are unable to make the choice themselves.

It is against the law in the UK but legal elsewhere, for example in the Netherlands and Switzerland. It can be voluntary, known as 'assisted suicide', or 'involuntary', which is when other people decide someone's life should end. However, withdrawal of treatment is not illegal in the UK and if the patient requests this then treatment must be stopped. This is called 'passive euthanasia'.

'Active euthanasia' is when deliberate action is taken to end life, using a lethal injection or administering a fatal dose of a drug. Many Christians would not differentiate between these ways of ending life arguing that, however good the motive, it is still killing. Christians often work to care for people who are dying by supporting the hospice movement.

RESEARCH NOTE

Find out about the work of Dame Cicely Saunders who founded the hospice movement.

The case of Dan James

In December 2008 23-year-old Dan James, who had broken his neck in a rugby accident in March 2007, ended his life, supported by his family, and helped by Dignitas, a Swiss clinic specialising in assisted suicide.

In an email to *Times Online* his mother, Julie, explains her decision to help Dan kill himself.

> *Three weeks ago our son was at last allowed his wish of a dignified death in the Dignitas apartment in Zurich. Dan was 23 years old and had broken his neck in a rugby accident in March 2007. He couldn't walk, had no hand function, but constant pain in all of his fingers. He was incontinent, suffered uncontrollable spasms in his legs and upper body and needed 24-hour care. Dan had tried to commit suicide three times but this was unsuccessful due to his disability. His only other option was to starve himself. Dan had been a lively and hugely active young man he was highly intelligent, lovable and so loved by his family. Whilst not everyone in Dan's situation would find it as unbearable as Dan, what right does any human being have to tell any other that they have to live such a life, filled with terror, discomfort and indignity, what right does one person who chooses to live with a particular illness or disability have to tell another that they should have to. .... Nobody but nobody should judge him or anyone else.*

Dan James (1985–2008).

Suicide

Suicide is when someone ends their own life. It is sometimes called 'self-murder' and was once treated as a crime. A person who tried to take their own life but failed could receive the death penalty. Roman Catholics believe it is a sin which would exclude someone from heaven. For a long time people who committed suicide were not allowed to be buried in the consecrated ground of churchyards. Today, although most Christians think it is morally wrong, their view has moved from being judgemental to being compassionate. People have a better understanding of the reasons why someone may want to end their own life, because they are very depressed, for example.

The Samaritans is an organisation set up in 1953 by Rev. Chad Varah, a Christian vicar, in the crypt of his London church, to provide 24-hour telephone counselling for people who feel suicidal and need someone to talk to. He started the Samaritans to 'befriend the suicidal and despairing', after conducting the funeral of a 13-year-old girl who had killed herself.

This is how his son Michael described their work: 'They give the sad person their total attention. They completely forget themselves. They listen... and listen... and listen without interrupting. We call them "Samaritans"'. Chad Varah died in 2007 but the Samaritan volunteers still provide a 24-hour service via phone, email, letter and face to face.

AO1+AO2 Skills ACTIVITIES

Sometimes a moral choice may be between two opposing goods rather than simply between right and wrong. This may be the case when someone is deciding whether to help another person end their life because it has become intolerable – what do you think?

Do animals have rights?

An artist's impression of the laboratory mouse grown by Dr Vacanti in 1995. The experiment was intended to show how replacement tissues can be grown to replace damaged human tissue.

Christian beliefs about the relationship between humans and animals

Christians believe that humans are made in the image of God. They are the most important part of creation and God gave them control over all other living things. This is based on Genesis 1:26 which describes how God gave humans power over all other living things. Most Christians believe that animals do not have souls and so cannot have the same relationship with God as humans. Therefore, some people believe that animals' lives have less importance than those of humans.

Most Christians see their role in relation to the natural world not as that of 'rulers' to control and exploit it but as stewards with a responsibility to care for and respect God's creation.

Jesus taught that God cares about the smallest creatures and that not one sparrow will fall to the ground without God knowing about it. He stressed that humans are worth more than sparrows and that God knows every hair on their heads (Matthew 10:29–30). Christians believe they should try to follow the example of a loving God, showing care and compassion.

AO2 skills ACTIVITIES

Work with a partner to create a mind map showing ways humans use animals. Use different colours to indicate uses which may exploit animals and those which promote a good relationship. Share your maps with the class.

RESEARCH NOTE

Research and prepare a short presentation about the lives of St Francis of Assisi and St Philip Neri and their treatment of animals.

> **Genesis 1:26a, 28**
>
> *Then God said, 'Let us make man in our image, in our likeness… God blessed them and said to them, "Be fruitful and increase in number; fill the earth and subdue it. Rule over the fish of the sea and the birds of the air and over every living thing that moves on the ground."'*

Christian beliefs about the use of animals in experiments

Although many Christians believe that animals do not have souls and are not aware of their existence in the same way as humans, they do not think it is acceptable to be cruel to animals. This would be a failure of their responsibility as stewards of God's creation. They would be showing a lack of respect for creation and, therefore, for God.

Christians recognise that humans can benefit from experiments on animals. For example, animal experiments led directly to the development of dialysis machines to treat kidney failure and to the development of drugs to prevent rejection in organ transplants. Such experiments were also central in creating vaccines for tuberculosis, which kills 3 million people every year.

Therefore, most Christians believe that it is acceptable to use animals for medical research if it is essential for the good of humans. However they stress that unnecessary suffering must be avoided, as causing pain to animals would not be compatible with living according to the teachings of Jesus. Most Christians would argue that if animal testing could result in a cure for a serious disease then it would be acceptable, provided as little suffering as possible was caused to the animal.

In 1995, Dr J. Vacanti, a transplant surgeon, grew what appeared to be a human ear onto the back of a mouse. When photos emerged the following year, they caused outrage among members of animal rights and pro-life groups who thought the mouse had been genetically engineered. In reality, the growth originated from cow cartilage (no human tissue was used) that was transplanted into the mouse, and was not the result of genetic engineering. Dr Vacanti said that the same technique might make it possible to grow a liver, saving the lives of people who die waiting for a liver transplant.

How far should we go?

The possibility of genetically modifying the bodies of animals so that they can be used to grow spare parts for humans also means that it is possible for scientists to create hybrid creatures. Patents for such developments have already been filed in the USA. What are the problems of such developments? What rights would they have?

REMEMBER THIS

Look back at the issues raised by the story of Frankenstein's monster in 2.2 to help you think about whether it is acceptable to use genetic engineering to create creatures for experiments.

AO2 skills ACTIVITIES

Is it natural for scientists to want to keep pushing the boundaries of what is possible? If so, what checks must be made to ensure that what is done is ethically acceptable? Just because we *can* do something, does that mean we *should*? *Who* decides and *how* do we decide?

Remember and Reflect

The questions in this section are based on the work you have done throughout this topic. Try to complete as many questions as you can.

The questions in set 1 are designed to test your factual recall and AO1 level skills (knowledge and understanding). The page numbers alongside the questions will help you to find information that might be useful for your answers. Use them to check what you have written.

The questions in set 2 are more challenging, using AO2 level skills (use of evidence and reasoned argument to evaluate personal responses and differing viewpoints). Your answers many come from more than one part of the topic.

AO1 Describe, explain and analyse, using knowledge and understanding

Find the answer on:

1 Explain what each of the following key words means. Use one sentence for each word.
  a abortion d sanctity of life
  b euthanasia e medical ethics
  c cloning f suicide
	PAGE 16

2 Give three examples of questions which focus on medical ethics.	**PAGE 18**
3 Give three legal reasons why a woman may have an abortion.	**PAGE 19**
4 Explain the Roman Catholic view on abortion and the reasons for it.	**PAGE 19**
5 Give two references to teachings in the Bible that a Christian might use to argue against abortion.	**PAGE 19**
6 Give two examples of fertility treatments and explain Christian views about whether they are acceptable or not.	**PAGE 20**
7 What is a 'spare embryo' and what problems does the use of spare embryos in medical research raise for Christians?	**PAGE 20**
8 Why do the issues raised by genetic engineering remind some people of the story of Frankenstein's monster?	**PAGE 21**
9 Why is euthanasia sometimes called 'mercy killing'?	**PAGE 22**
10 Explain why Christians might have different opinions about euthanasia.	**PAGE 22–23**
11 'The Lord gave and the Lord has taken away, may the name of the Lord be praised' (Job 1:21b). Why are these words often used at Christian funerals? How do they support the view of some Christians that euthanasia and suicide are wrong?	**PAGE 22–23**
12 Give an example of how Christians might try to support and care for people who are dying.	**PAGE 22**
13 What do Christians believe about the relationship between humans and animals? Explain how they justify their view by referring to teachings, from the Bible.	**PAGE 24**
14 Give two examples of how experiments on animals have led to life-saving treatments for humans.	**PAGE 25**

AO2 Use evidence and reasoned argument to express and evaluate personal responses, informed insights, and differing viewpoints

1 Why do you think the beginning and end of life poses so many difficult questions for religious people, philosophers and people with no religious beliefs?

2 'Abortion is murder!' How would you respond to someone who holds this view? Explain the reasons for your response.

3 Do you think that women who claim that they have the right to treat their body however they choose should include the need to treat it responsibly by preventing the risk of unwanted pregnancy? Explain your reasons.

4 'Humans should always protect and preserve life and never destroy it.' Do you agree or disagree? Explain your reasons.

5 'Embryo research is so important in finding treatments for some terrible illnesses Christians should encourage it.' Do you agree? Give reasons to support your answer and show you have thought about different points of view.

6 Is the argument 'We should because we can' an acceptable argument for supporting cloning and other aspects of genetic engineering? Give clear reasons to support your view.

7 'Animals do not have rights but humans have a moral responsibility to treat them properly.' Discuss this statement referring to Christian beliefs and your own views, giving reasons for them.

8 Think back over the issues you have studied in this topic. What do you think is the most difficult question for medical ethics and why?

Welcome to the Grade Studio

Grade Studio is here to help you improve your grades by working through typical questions you might find on an examination paper. For a full explanation of how this feature works and how exam questions are structured, see page 14. For a full explanation of Assessment Objectives and Levels of Response, see pages x–xi in the Introduction.

AO1

Question

Explain Christian attitudes to the use of animals in medical research.　　　　　　　**[6 marks]**

Student's answer

Christians believe that God placed humans in charge of the world and in charge of the animals.

Some Christians believe that, because humanity was placed in charge of the animals, we can eat them and do anything else that we wish with them. Their life is not as valuable as human life, so if animals can help save human lives, this is a good reason to conduct medical research on them.

Examiner's comment

The candidate has given a satisfactory answer to the question. There are two relevant points, but they are not explained in any detail. In order to reach Level 3, the answer needs to give more information and examples. The candidate could also use more technical terms from the specification to show the breadth of their knowledge and understanding.

Student's improved answer

Christians believe that God placed humans in charge of the world and in charge of the animals. Some Christians believe that, because humanity was placed in charge of the animals, we can eat them and do anything else that we wish with them. Their life is not as valuable as human life, so if animals can help save human lives, this is a good reason to conduct medical research on them.

Some Christians might say that this is using animals as a type of lesser creation, and that there is no basis for this. In fact, God placed a responsibility on people to look after creation known as stewardship and misusing animals goes against this. Many Christians are also concerned as to what experiments take place on animals. While some people may be reasonably happy with experiments on animals that lead to cures for human diseases, especially if there is no other way of carrying out the research, they may be much less happy with experiments to test cosmetics or other tests which are not necessary and are simply taking place for human convenience. Many Christians believe that the responsible thing to do is to try to find ways of researching cures for disease using as few animals as possible.

Examiner's comment

This is now a good answer to the question. The candidate has shown a clear understanding of the question. There is good description and explanation of a variety of different responses that Christians might have in relation to animals. The candidate has shown good analysis in dealing with the question of experiments on animals. The information is presented clearly and there is good use of technical terms.

Question

'Every woman has the right to have a baby.' Discuss this statement. You should include different, supported points of view and a personal viewpoint. You must refer to Christianity in your answer. **[12 marks]**

Student's answer

Christians might say that women are designed by God to have babies and that therefore every woman has the right to have one. Some Christians might also say that, if a woman is not able to have a baby by natural means, she should be able to have fertility treatment because God has enabled scientists to discover this. God tells people in the Old Testament to multiply so every woman has a right to if they are able.

Examiner's comment

The candidate has given a limited answer to the question. There are two relevant points but neither is expanded very far. In order to reach Level 4 the answer needs to give alternative viewpoints and to include a personal response.

Student's improved answer

Christians might say that women are designed by God to have babies and that therefore every woman has the right to have one. Some Christians might also say that, if a woman is not able to have a baby by natural means, she should be able to have fertility treatment because God has enabled scientists to discover this. God tells people in the Old Testament to multiply, so every woman has a right to if they are able.

Other Christians might say that a baby is a gift, not a right, and that if God wanted a woman to have a baby then she would have one. The fact that she cannot conceive naturally means that she was not intended to have a baby. God has other plans for her rather than being a mother. Others may say that this sort of statement means that single mothers and lesbians would also have the right to have babies, and they would not approve of this because the baby will not be brought up in a traditional family unit. I find it difficult to decide about this issue.

My personal opinion is that there is no simple answer to this question. I do understand that many women are desperate to have a baby and may not be able to have one naturally, so they will want fertility treatment. However, it is also true that there are a lot of questions to be answered about single women choosing to have a baby without a father.

Examiner's comment

This is now a good answer to the question. The candidate has shown a clear understanding of the question and has presented a range of views supported by evidence and argument. The answer explains Christian views, amongst others, and includes a personal viewpoint, which is also supported.

These specimen answers provide an outline of how you could construct your response. Space does not allow us to give a full response. The examiner will be looking for more detail in your actual exam responses.

Topic 3: Religion, poverty and wealth

The Big Picture

In this Topic, you will be addressing religious beliefs and teachings about:

- Christian views of wealth and the causes of hunger, poverty and disease
- what the Bible says about concern for others, and different ways in which Christians might put charity into practice
- Christian teachings about the use of money, and donating to charity
- Christian teachings about moral and immoral occupations and the impact these teachings have on believers.

You will also think about the ways in which these beliefs affect the life and outlook of Christians in today's world.

DID YOU KNOW?

- According to the charity Shelter 3.8 million children in the UK live in poverty once their housing costs have been paid.
- According to the UN 25,000 people die every day of hunger or hunger-related causes, despite there being enough food in the world to feed everyone.
- The charity Christian Aid gave more than £66 million in aid to more than 50 countries, including the UK.
- Christian charities such as CAFOD and Christian Aid help people of any religion and those who do not follow a religion.

KEY WORDS

charity To give help or money to those in need.

compassion Sympathy and concern for others.

ecumenical Different Christian denominations working together.

immoral Not conforming to accepted standards of behaviour.

LEDC Less economically developed country.

MEDC More economically developed country.

moral Conforming to accepted standards of behaviour.

philanthropist Someone who donates money, goods, services or time to help a cause which benefits society.

tithe The Christian practice of giving a tenth of their income to charity.

trade restrictions Restrictions made by one country about the amounts and types of goods it will allow into the country from other countries.

In 1984, 1989 and 2004 many famous singers came together to perform concerts and record songs to raise awareness of poverty in African countries. What are the advantages and disadvantages of such large and irregular campaigns?

Christian beliefs about the causes of hunger, poverty and disease

What does Christianity say about the causes of hunger, poverty and disease?

The next two pages will help you to:

- explain Christian beliefs about the causes of hunger, poverty and disease
- reflect on your own responses to these issues.

Hunger

Many **more economically developed countries** (MEDCs) have **trade restrictions**, or taxes, which prevent **less economically developed countries** (LEDCs) from selling high-value processed goods to them. This means that, for example, an LEDC can sell raw coffee beans to an MEDC at a low price. The coffee beans are then processed into instant coffee by a manufacturer from the MEDC and sold on for a much higher price. However if the LEDC tried to process and sell instant coffee the **trade restrictions**, or taxes, would mean they were unable to make even a small profit.

Many large companies based in MEDCs set up factories in LEDCs, where wages are much lower, to maximise their profits. In some of these factories the working conditions are so poor that they would not be allowed to operate in the UK.

Many Christians feel it is unfair for MEDCs to prevent LEDCs from developing a more profitable economy, or to exploit their workers. Traidcraft is a Christian organisation which aims to bring about fairer trade practices, and reduce poverty by supplying fair trade products to the UK.

Some Christians may believe that hunger in the world is largely brought about by the greed of certain countries at the expense of others. They may also refer to teachings such as the parable of The Sheep and the Goats (Matthew 25:31–46) as an example of how Christians should treat people less fortunate than themselves.

ACTIVITIES

AO1 skills

Working in pairs, consider why some people are very poor and some are very rich. Make a list of possible reasons then share them with the class.

A child in a slum city in India.

RESEARCH NOTE

Visit the Traidcraft website and find out how buying fair trade products helps people in LEDCs.

Poverty

In the past MEDCs encouraged LEDCs to borrow money from them. The interest rates then increased, and the LEDCs have sometimes been unable to repay the loan. In some cases the original amount of the loan has been paid back many times over, but because the interest is added the loans are still not paid off.

Some Christians might feel that the practices used in loaning money to LEDCs amount to usury. Usury can mean loaning money at any interest rate, but is usually interpreted by Christians today as charging interest at an unfairly high rate. Usury is forbidden in the Old Testament, and the Prophet Ezekiel considered it as bad as robbery.

Although many Christians do borrow and lend money they still believe that this should not be done at the expense of the poor. The gospels are full of examples and teachings about caring for the poor and this is a central part of Christian belief and practice.

> **Ezekiel 18:8–9**
> *He does not lend at usury or take excessive interest.*

Natural disasters

Many parts of the world are subject to natural disasters, such as floods, droughts, hurricanes and volcanic eruptions. In LEDCs such events are more likely to lead to death because these countries cannot afford to take the same kind of preventative measures as MEDCs, and do not have access to the same kind of emergency services.

In the past some Christians tended to see natural disasters as punishments for not being faithful to God. Today some still see natural disasters as being performed by the Devil. They might believe the Devil is trying to make people feel God is not helping them, to destroy their faith.

However, many Christians might point to the role humans play in natural disasters. For example, heavy rain may cause flooding where forests have been cut down to make quick profits. These Christians might then point to the selfishness of those who make a profit for themselves without thinking about the impact of their actions on the world as a whole.

Disease

In some countries children are more likely to die of diseases such as measles because there is no vaccination programme. In other countries, lack of access to clean drinking water means people die of diseases such as cholera. The World Health Organisation (WHO) in 2003 estimated that of the 6 million people with HIV/AIDS in LEDCs, only 300,000 were actually receiving treatment.

Some Christians feel that the poverty which prevents people accessing healthcare is unacceptable, and call for drug companies to make their products available more cheaply in poorer countries.

As with poverty most Christians would see the causes of disease as being the result of the exploitation of the poor. However, in the time of the New Testament it was believed that some illnesses were the result of sin. When Jesus healed a blind man he said: 'Receive your sight; your faith has healed you' (Luke 18:42b).

FOR DEBATE

Some baby products have recently offered to donate the cost of a tetanus vaccination (approximately 86p) to a well-known charity for every specially marked product sold. Is this a good way to help LEDCs?

AO2 skills ACTIVITIES

Create a mind map showing all the factors which contribute to hunger, poverty and disease. Highlight those causes which could be changed by individual action in one colour, and those which need changes by governments and organisations in another. How might a Christian try to respond to these issues?

Religious views of poverty and wealth

The next two pages will help you to:

- explain Christian attitudes to wealth and the use of money
- explain Christian responses to poverty
- identify and reflect on your own views about issues to do with wealth and poverty.

Christian attitudes to wealth and poverty

Many Christians do not see a problem with being wealthy, but they do believe that wealth should be used appropriately. However, they also believe that it is part of the Christian duty to help people who are less fortunate than themselves.

Some Christians see wealth as a temptation which leads some people to behave in a less Christian manner, so they believe that wealth needs to be handled with care. If wealth is used in an appropriate manner then heaven will still be accessible.

What does the Bible say about wealth and poverty?

Throughout the Bible there are teachings about wealth and poverty in both the Old and New Testaments. People are encouraged to look after the poor:

Deuteronomy 15:11

There will always be poor people in the land. Therefore I command you to be open handed toward your brothers and toward the poor and needy in your land.

This is seen as a form of worship:

Proverbs 14:31

He who oppresses the poor shows contempt for their Maker, but whoever is kind to the needy honours God.

People are also warned of the dangers of loving money as it can interfere with loving God:

Matthew 6:24

No one can serve two masters. Either he will hate the one and love the other, or he will be devoted to the one and despise the other. You cannot serve both God and Money.

Matthew 19:24

Again I tell you it is easier for a camel to go through the eye of a needle than for a rich man to enter the kingdom of God.

ACTIVITIES

Look carefully at the Bible quotes on this page. What attitudes to wealth and poverty do they show? How might these views affect the ways in which Christians see wealth and poverty today?

FOR DEBATE

Do you think being wealthy makes it harder to be good?

Jesus answered:

> **Matthew 19:21**
> *If you want to be perfect, go, sell your possessions and give to the poor, and you will have treasure in heaven. Then come, follow me.*

Finally, people are warned that they must acquire money honestly:

> **Proverbs 13:11**
> *Dishonest money dwindles away but he who gathers money little by little makes it grow.*

The Bristol City Museum and Art Gallery.

How have some Christians used their wealth?

In Edinburgh in the 1800s the Nelsons (a Christian family), who made their money from printing and publishing, built four libraries for the use of working men, and contributed to the building of the Royal Infirmary.

In the second half of the 19th century, in the UK, Thomas Barnardo, with the financial support of other Christian **philanthropists**, such as Lord Shaftesbury, set up a series of homes to help destitute children. The organisation he founded still exists today helping children and their families.

In the 1800s and 1900s the Wills family in Bristol, who had made their fortune in tobacco, made generous donations to Bristol University and to the City's Museum and Art Gallery.

In November 2008 Christian philanthropists offered £90,000 to support five Christian charities following a 'Dragons' Den' style presentation.

What do the Churches say about wealth today?

Christian Action on Poverty (CAP) is an **ecumenical** group set up to address the issues of poverty in the UK. In the past they have encouraged Christians to live on the minimum wage during the 40 days of Lent, to develop their understanding of poverty, and to donate any money they have saved to organisations which reduce poverty.

In 2006 Pope Benedict XVI argued that LEDCs should be allowed to trade more fairly with MEDCs so that they could generate more wealth and reduce poverty. In 2008 the Bishop of Rochester, the Right Reverend Dr Nazir-Ali, argued that high earners should be sharing their wealth with others rather than simply trying to make more money for themselves.

REMEMBER THIS

Ecumenical refers to a situation where people from churches of different denominations work together.

ACTIVITIES

Do you think Christian teachings on wealth and poverty are fair?

How do you feel about the fact that some people have so much money when others are dying through lack of food or clean water?

Concern for others

The next two pages will help you to:

- explain Christian teaching about caring for people in need
- explore how Christians might put these teachings into practice
- identify and reflect on your own views on charity.

AO1 skills **ACTIVITIES**

Find out more about the work of one of these charities – CAFOD, Christian Aid, Tear Fund or Traidcraft. How does their work reflect Christian teachings? Is their work an effective way of putting Christian teachings into practice?

The Salvation Army work to help the poor and homeless.

What are the Christian teachings about caring for those in need?

The Bible is quite clear that Christians have a duty to support the poor. Look at the teachings below and consider how they might be put into practice.

These teachings are found in the Old Testament as well as the New Testament. The first text shows that people who do not care for the poor will suffer themselves:

Proverbs 21:13

If a man shuts his ears to the cry of the poor, he too will cry out and not be answered.

1 John 3:17–18

If anyone has material possessions and sees his brother in need but has no pity on him, how can the love of God be in him? Dear children, let us not love with words or tongue but with actions and in truth.

Christians are told that they should give money privately and not advertise their generosity:

RESEARCH NOTE

Read the parable of The Sheep and the Goats in Matthew 25. What implications does this have for Christians about how they should behave?

> **Matthew 6:2**
>
> *So when you give to the needy, do not announce it with trumpets, as the hypocrites do in the synagogues and on the streets, to be honoured by men. I tell you the truth, they have received their reward in full.*

These teachings clearly show that Christians should help the poor and show **compassion**. However, they should do so discreetly, and not in such a way as to attract undue attention to their deeds. It is the fact that they have helped the poor which is important, not that they receive recognition for doing so.

> **Mark 12:42–43**
>
> *But a poor widow came and put in two very small copper coins, worth only a fraction of a penny.*
> *Calling his disciples to him, Jesus said, 'I tell you the truth, this poor widow has put more into the treasury than all the others'.*

This final passage shows that the size of what is given is not important. It is the intention and cost to the giver which is more significant.

How do Christians put these teachings into practice?

In the Old Testament a tenth (or **tithe**) of the harvest was given to God's work. Some Christians today still donate a percentage of their income to **charity**. They might donate this money to their church, or give it to charity. Some Christians donate this money to a Christian charity such as CAFOD or Christian Aid. There is no requirement to do this however, and some may donate their money to non-Christian charities which help others.

For some Christians donating money can be hard, especially if they are poor themselves. They may still feel a duty to help others however. They could do this by donating their time or their expertise. They might for example volunteer in a charity shop or help at a homeless shelter. They could also help teach young previously homeless people how to cook, or provide knitted goods to help those in other countries.

The Salvation Army is a Christian denomination which places a great emphasis on helping those in need. They often raise money by playing in brass bands in town centres. This money is then used to provide homeless shelters, counselling for drug and alcohol abuse and basic equipment kits to help people who were homeless and are moving into rented accommodation.

Some Christians feel the need to be more involved in helping others. They might work for a charitable organisation full time. For some Christians their whole life becomes dedicated to helping those in need. Jackie Pullinger was a Christian who went to Hong Kong as a missionary. She was so distressed by the suffering of drug addicts there that she worked to set up homes where they could withdraw from the drugs and get help in readjusting to normal life. Some Christians get involved in political campaigns in order to try and bring about change which benefits those in need.

FOR DEBATE

'When you mix politics and religion, you get politics.' Discuss this statement.
Should Christians get involved in political action, or should they leave politics to the politicians?

AO2 skills ACTIVITIES

Should the poor have to rely on charities to help them or should society be fairer to everyone in the first place?

Religion, poverty and wealth

The next two pages will help you to:

- explain why some ways of earning a living are not acceptable to Christians
- evaluate your own views about moral and immoral ways of earning a living.

AO1+AO2 Skills **ACTIVITIES**

Make two lists: one showing jobs that you think are moral, the other showing those you think are immoral. Look at the lists again after reading these two pages. Do you think a Christian would agree with your lists? Make any additions or changes you think a Christian might make in a different coloured pen.

Many Christians do not approve of gambling.

Concept of moral and immoral

When people use the words **moral** and **immoral** they are usually talking about things which they consider to be good or bad, good or evil or right and wrong. These may be things which people just 'know' are right or wrong, or things which a religion says are right or wrong.

Moral and immoral occupations

Many people might have an instinctive idea of jobs which they would consider to be immoral because they hurt or exploit others. For Christians their concept of what jobs are immoral is also likely to be influenced by the Bible.

The Bible does not list moral and immoral occupations, but its teachings about how to treat others can be used to help determine whether a job would be immoral. One example is the teaching in the Bible against usury which might lead Christians to believe that working for a debt consolidation company (who charge higher than usual rates of interest to those whose loans have become unmanageable) would be immoral.

Some Christians use the second of the 'Two Great Commandments' in Mark as their guideline about whether an occupation is moral or immoral. This says people should love their neighbour as themselves. This might then imply that if an occupation could harm others then it would be immoral. This could be easily applied to occupations which directly cause harm to others, for example pornography, or gambling which causes most gamblers to lose money.

What is more difficult to assess is how far people should take this, for example should a Christian reject a job working for a fishing magazine because the same publisher also publishes pornography? Should they refuse to work for a major chocolate manufacturer because they buy cocoa beans in a way which exploits cocoa workers? Would working for a drug manufacturer which conducted human tests in LEDCs be acceptable? There are no straightforward answers to these questions, and individual Christians have to come to their own conclusions.

There are however occupations which clearly uphold the Great Commandments, and these might be deemed by Christians as moral. They are often jobs in the 'caring' professions, where the work carried out can be seen to have a direct impact on people's lives. They include teaching, medicine, social services and most **charity** work. Some other occupations might fall into this category as without them people's lives might be very difficult or dangerous. This might include refuse collectors, cleaners, and people working in the court systems, or the fire services.

Impacts of these teachings on believers

Although Christians will always try to live by the teachings of the Bible, there may be situations in which they find it very difficult to know what to do. The Bible might indicate that an occupation is immoral. This might be something which most people agree is immoral or it might be something rather different, like working with battery hens which the individual Christian might think was cruel. Sometimes people who have to earn a living and support their families may find that they have to compromise their beliefs in order to survive.

> ### Mark 12:29–31
> 'The most important one,' answered Jesus, 'is this: "Hear, O Israel, the Lord our God, the Lord is one. Love the Lord your God with all your heart and with all your soul and with all your mind and with all your strength." The second is this: "Love your neighbour as yourself." There is no commandment greater than these.'

ACTIVITIES

'Christians should be prepared to take any job rather than be unemployed.' Discuss this statement. You should include different, supported points of view and a personal viewpoint.

Remember and Reflect

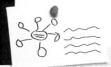

The questions in this section are based on the work you have done throughout this topic. Try to complete as many questions as you can.

The questions in set 1 are designed to test your factual recall and AO1 level skills (knowledge and understanding). The page numbers alongside the questions will help you to find information that might be useful for your answers. Use them to check against what you have written.

The questions in set 2 are more challenging, using AO2 level skills (use of evidence and reasoned argument to evaluate personal responses and differing viewpoints). Your answers many come from more than one part of the topic.

AO1 Describe, explain and analyse, using knowledge and understanding

Find the answer on:

1 List three causes of poverty.	**PAGE 32–33**
2 What is usury?	**PAGE 33**
3 Give two reasons why Christians might be unhappy with the poverty in LEDCs.	**PAGE 32–33**
4 Explain why LEDCs are more likely to be harmed by natural disasters than MEDCs.	**PAGE 33**
5 Give one Biblical teaching about wealth and explain what it means.	**PAGE 34**
6 Why might Christians think being wealthy leads to temptation?	**PAGE 34**
7 Give one example of a Christian who has used their wealth to help others.	**PAGE 35**
8 Explain how the Christian Action on Poverty (CAP) practice of living on the minimum wage during Lent might help Christians develop empathy for the poor.	**PAGE 35**
9 Explain in 50 words what the Bible says about helping the poor.	**PAGE 36–37**
10 Give the names of two Christian charities.	**PAGE 36**
11 What is a tithe?	**PAGE 37**
12 How might those with little money care for those in need?	**PAGE 37**
13 What does the Bible say about moral and immoral occupations?	**PAGE 39**
14 Construct a chart like the one below showing what Christians might consider moral and immoral occupations and why.	**PAGE 39**

Moral occupations	Why?	Immoral occupations	Why?

AO2 Use evidence and reasoned argument to express and evaluate personal responses, informed insights, and differing viewpoints

1 'It is the responsibility of LEDCs to sort out their own problems.' Discuss this statement. You should include different, supported points of view and a personal viewpoint. You must refer to Christianity in your answer.

2 Construct an argument showing the benefits of accumulating wealth so one can then help other people.

3 'People who gather great riches are selfish.' Discuss this statement. You should include different, supported points of view and a personal viewpoint. You must refer to Christianity in your answer.

4 Create a chart like the one below showing the advantages and disadvantages of charities helping people in need.

Advantages	Disadvantages

Now explain whether you think charities should help those in need or not.

5 'Giving money to charity is not doing enough to help those in need.' Discuss this statement. You should include different, supported points of view and a personal viewpoint. You must refer to Christianity in your answer.

6 Copy and complete the chart below to help you give supported evidence for or against the statements in the chart.

	How a Christian might respond	Evidence to support their views
'Any job is better than none.'		
'No Christian should ever work for a gambling organisation.'		
'I can't work in my local newsagent – it sells pornography.'		

Welcome to the Grade Studio

Grade Studio is here to help you improve your grades by working through typical questions you might find on an examination paper. For a full explanation of how this feature works and how exam questions are structured, see page 14. For a full explanation of Assessment Objectives and Levels of Response, see pages x–xi in the Introduction.

AO1

Question

Why might Christians give money to charity?   **[6 marks]**

Student's answer

Christians are nice people who want others to like them, so they will always give money to charity. Christians also believe that the Bible says they must give to charity.

Some Christians give money in church every Sunday when there is a collection so that the church can work to help others. They do this because Jesus praised people who helped others.

Examiner's comment

The candidate has given a satisfactory answer to the question. The opening sentence is very weak. There are two relevant points but neither is explained in any detail. In order to reach Level 3 the candidate needs to give more information and examples. The candidate could also use more technical terms from the specification to show the breadth of their knowledge and understanding.

Student's improved answer

Christians are nice people who want others to like them, so they will always give money to charity. Christians also believe that the Bible says they must give to charity.

Some Christians give money in church every Sunday when there is a collection so that the church can work to help others. They do this because Jesus praised people who helped others.

Some people, as well as giving to a weekly collection, may also give a tenth of their income to the church to help the less fortunate – this is called tithing. Charity has always been part of Christian life and teaching since the time of the deacons in Jerusalem who looked after the widows. Also, Jesus told the Parable of the Widow's Mite where a widow gave a tiny amount, but it was really all she had, as an example of how and why people should give to charity. He also told the rich young ruler to sell all his possessions and give the money to the poor. By giving money to charity, Christians are following Jesus' teaching and example.

Examiner's comment

This is now a good answer to the question. The candidate has shown a clear understanding of the question. There is good description and explanation of a variety of different reasons why Christians might give to charity. The candidate has shown some analysis. The information is presented clearly and there is good use of technical terms.

Question

'People must look after their family before they worry about the poor.' Discuss this statement. You should include different, supported points of view and a personal viewpoint. You must refer to Christianity in your answer. **[12 marks]**

Student's answer

The proverb says 'charity begins at home', so of course people should look after their own family first.

Some Christians might also say that their family is their first responsibility and so they must look after the needs of their family before they can worry about people outside of it. The Bible is clear about the responsibilty of parents towards their children, so the family must come first.

Examiner's comment

The candidate has given a limited answer to the question. There are two points but they both address the same point of view and neither is expanded. In order to reach Level 4 the candidate needs to give alternative viewpoints and also include a personal response.

Student's improved answer

The proverb says 'charity begins at home', so of course people should look after their own family first. Some Christians might also say that their family is their first responsibility and so they must look after the needs of their family before they can worry about people outside of it. The Bible is clear about the responsibilty of parents towards their children, so the family must come first.

Some people, on the other hand, might think that because of the amount of suffering, disease and poverty in the world, as Christians they have an obligation to look after the poor. Jesus told his followers to look after the poor and not to concern themselves with their own wellbeing. He asked his Disciples to leave their family and follow him and put others before their family. The parable of The Sheep and the Goats makes it clear that God will judge people by how they helped othes who are in need. I think the statement is correct.

My personal opinion is that Christians have to strike a balance between the two positions. Of course, they have to look after their family but, if they are thinking of spending money on things that are simply luxuries, they need to be concerned about doing something for the poor first.

Examiner's comment

This is now a good answer to the question. The candidate has shown a clear understanding of the question and has presented a range of views supported by evidence and argument. The answer explains Christian views, amongst others, and includes a personal viewpoint, which is also supported.

These specimen answers provide an outline of how you could construct your response. Space does not allow us to give a full response. The examiner will be looking for more detail in your actual exam responses.

Topic 4: Responsibility for the planet

The Big Picture

In this Topic, you will be addressing religious beliefs and teachings about:

- the origins of the world and life
- people and animals
- environmental issues.

You will also think about the ways in which these beliefs affect the life and outlook of Christians in today's world.

DID YOU KNOW?

- Scientists believe it is possible to hear echoes of the Big Bang today. The hiss left over from collapsed stars (pulsars) can be picked up by radio telescopes such as the one at Jodrell Bank.

- Some Christians calculate that the world began in 4004 BCE. They use evidence in the Bible, derived from the ages of various Old Testament people to calculate this. Calculations do vary and some Christians date the beginning of the world as far back as 10,000 years.

- We share 99.4 per cent of our DNA with chimpanzees. They experience a range of emotions, have a similar life span and form strong family ties.

- There is no fossil evidence of the direct descent of humans from apes. Fossil evidence of early humans has been found which is believed to date around 6 million years BCE but what has not yet been found is fossil evidence of skeletons that show a transition from apes to humans.

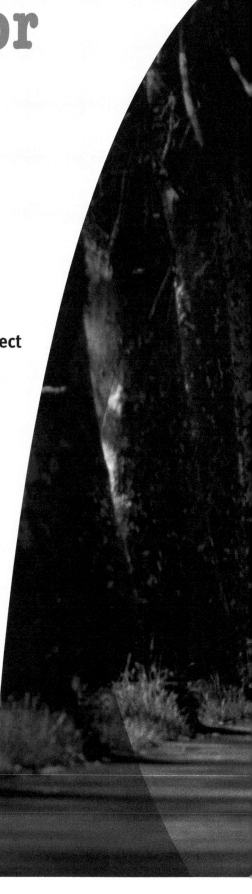

Big Bang theory The scientific theory that the universe came into being as a result of a cosmic explosion.

Creationists Christians who believe that the creation of the universe happened in exactly the way Genesis describes it.

Darwinism The theory Charles Darwin put forward for evolution.

environmental issues A concern for the way humans exploit natural resources.

evolution The way in which animals and plants adapt to their surroundings – the survival of the fittest.

Intelligent Design theory The idea that the complexity of life on earth and the fact that conditions on earth are just right for life prove that it must have had a designer.

natural selection The way animals and plants adapt to life or die out.

pollution Destruction of the natural world by human activity.

GET STARTED

As a class consider who has the most right to say what happens to a rainforest. Should it be:

- indigenous people who need more land to grow food
- the government in the countries concerned
- consumers in the western world who want cheap real wood furniture
- religious people who believe it is wrong to destroy God's creation
- environmentalists who are concerned about the long-term care of the planet?

Rank them in the order the class decides and put the reasons against each.

If the earth is God's creation then what responsibility do humans have for it?

Christian teachings about the origins of the world and humanity

The next two pages will help you to:

- explore Christian teachings about the origins of the world
- identify Christian teachings about the origins of humanity
- evaluate Christian interpretations of the Genesis story.

Christian teachings about the origin of the world

The Bible says 'In the beginning, God created the heavens and the earth' (Genesis 1.1) and goes on to explain in detail that God created everything in existence out of nothing or from chaos.

- **Day 1**: God created earth and night and day.
- **Day 2**: God created the sea and sky.
- **Day 3**: God created plant life.
- **Day 4**: God created the sun and stars.
- **Day 5**: God created fish and birds saying 'Let the water teem with living creatures, and let birds fly above the earth across the expanse of the sky.'
- **Day 6**: God said 'Let the land produce living creatures according to their kind: livestock, creatures that move along the ground, and wild animals, each according to its kind... Let us make man in our own image, in our likeness... God saw all that he had made, and it was very good.'
- **Day 7**: God had finished all the work he had been doing, so on the seventh day he rested from all his work and made the seventh day holy.

AO1 skills **ACTIVITIES**

Make a chart to show the different Christian interpretations of the Genesis story of the origins of the world. Leave a column on the chart so you can add what these Christians think about scientific theories of creation and evolution.

One story but several interpretations

All Christians believe the Bible is telling them that the world was created by God as an act of love, but they differ in their interpretation of the Genesis story. For some Christians the Biblical story is a factual account of how God made the universe, the Earth and all life on it. They believe it is true because the Bible says: 'Thus the heavens and earth were completed in all their vast array.' For them, the Bible is the Word of God and everything written there is literally true.

Christians who believe the Genesis story of creation word for word are called **Creationists.** They say God created life out of nothing in six days, each 24 hours long. Because God is all-powerful, a feat like that is not at all impossible. Using information in Genesis and elsewhere in the Bible some calculate that the creation of the earth took place around 6000 years ago.

Others believe the Bible is teaching them that God created the world and describing the order in which he went about it. They do not think each day of creation literally means 24 hours. The word 'day' is being used to mean a period of time which could be a million years. It is rather like when we say 'in the olden days'. Day can also be translated from the Hebrew as aeon or age. Whilst the story is not to be taken literally, it gives Christians a clear idea of who the creator was and how creation occurred.

For other Christians the Genesis story is just a story told to people in a pre-scientific age to help them understand why the world came into being. It was never intended as a scientific account and certainly should not be taken literally. Like all fables it has a meaning at its heart, which is that everything in existence was created by God out of nothing.

Christian teachings about the origins of humanity

On the sixth day of creation after God had created the animals the Bible says 'So God created man in his own image, in the image of God he created him; male and female he created them' (Genesis 1:27). Genesis 2 gives more detail of the creation of humanity. Here it says God created Adam then formed Eve from his rib bone. These were the first two people from whom the rest of humanity are descended.

Creationists have no problem accepting both Genesis accounts of the creation of humanity as fact. For them the Bible stories show that humans were created by God, quite separately from the animal kingdom. These stories teach Creationists that people were created in the image of God which enables them to have a personal relationship with God. This makes human life special and sacred.

Other Christians believe the Biblical account of human creation is telling them that God deliberately created people to be like him and to have a special relationship with their creator. They do not accept the story of Adam and Eve in the Garden of Eden as a factual account of the way humans came to be on the earth.

Some Christians dismiss all the writings in Genesis as myths handed down from a primitive society. They do not think there is anything scientific in it, it is simply telling people about their relationship with God and the environment.

FOR DEBATE

With a partner discuss the strengths and weaknesses of the different Christian interpretations of the Genesis story. How would you interpret the story and why?

Religion and science

The next two pages will help you to:

- analyse religious understandings of the origin of the world in relation to scientific theories
- evaluate religious understandings of the origins of humanity in relation to scientific theories.

Did humans evolve from apes?

What does science say about the origin of the world?

Latest scientific thinking says the universe began with the **Big Bang** between 12 and 20 billion years ago. Before that nothing existed. Scientists believe evidence of the Big Bang can be found in our continually expanding universe which can be dated by measuring the red shift in stars. Geological evidence from rocks shows the Earth is around 4 billion years old, far older than the six thousand years some **Creationists** calculate from Biblical accounts.

Are Christians and scientists in conflict?

Those Christians who see the Genesis story as a myth written for primitive people have no problem in accepting the Big Bang theory. For them the Big Bang was God's method of bringing the world into being. Like scientists, these Christians agree that the Big Bang created a universe out of nothing.

RESEARCH NOTE

Go to Jodrell Bank's website to listen to the sound of pulsars, which are evidence of the Big Bang, and the Natural History Museum's website to look at fossil evidence for the links between early man and apes. How convinced are you by these pieces of evidence? Why?

An intelligent designer?

Some Christians believe in the **Intelligent Design** theory. They accept the Big Bang theory as the method used to create the planet and they accept that **evolution** led to humanity developing from earlier life forms. However, these Christians do not think this was the result of random chance because life forms are extremely complex. They argue there must be intelligence behind such complexity. That intelligence must be God. ↳ cosmology

Some scientists have commented that the odds on the exact conditions for the Big Bang occurring by chance were about as likely as a tornado sweeping through a scrap yard and creating a jumbo jet.

Creationists reject the Big Bang theory totally because it conflicts with the Genesis accounts, but they attempt to use scientific evidence to prove that biblical accounts are true. For instance, fossils found in the Grand Canyon suggest that there was a great flood, which Creationists argue is the one in Genesis 7 when Noah built an ark. Creationists also argue that the Genesis story is supported by scientific knowledge, showing that it is impossible for living matter to develop from non-living matter. They say that creation has to have a creator, and that is God.

Evolution or not?

In the past many people accepted that the story of God creating Adam and Eve in Genesis 2 was a factual account of the creation of human life. It was Charles Darwin's book, *On the Origin of Species*, published in 1859, which altered things. He produced evidence that showed birds and animals had adapted to their environment. From this he deduced that humans had evolved from apes and were not created as a separate species.

Creationists, who believe the Bible is the word of God, totally reject other ideas. They argue that humans were created separately by God. Darwin's idea of **natural selection**, which is often called 'survival of the fittest', is not likely to be the work of a loving God because it involves suffering and death as the strong kill the weak in order to survive.

Other Christians have no problem accepting Darwin's account of evolution by natural selection. In their view humanity has evolved into a species that is separate from other animals because of its superior intelligence and possession of emotions. They argue that 'made in the image of God' should be interpreted to mean God wants humans to grow more like him and have a personal relationship with him.

Not all Christians accept **Darwinism** in its entirety. Whilst some accept the concept of evolution, they point out that no fossil evidence has yet appeared showing the direct descent of humans from apes, the so-called 'missing link'. Maybe humanity was indeed a separate species.

FOR DEBATE

Some people would say that scientific theories totally contradict the Genesis story. Do you agree? Would you call the Intelligent Design theory scientific or not? Why?

AO2 skills ACTIVITIES

Make a Venn diagram to compare the views of Creationists, scientists who are atheist, and Christians who accept scientific evidence about the origins of the planet and human life. Notice where the views overlap. Where would you place yourself on this diagram and why?

The place of humanity in relation to animals

The next two pages will help you to:

- explore the place of humanity in relation to animals
- analyse attitudes to animals and their treatment
- evaluate human treatment of animals.

RESEARCH NOTE

Research the life of St Francis of Assisi to find out why he is the patron saint of animals.

Humans share 99.4% of their DNA with chimpanzees.

Humanity is at the top of creation

The Genesis story clearly sets out the relationship between humans and animals.

Most Christians accept that humanity is the most important part of God's creation. The first story in the book of Genesis says that animals were created first and God made humans afterwards. This shows Christians that humanity is both distinct from animal life and superior to it.

The Genesis story goes on to say God brought all the animals he had created to Adam, so Adam could name them. Christians see this as further evidence of human superiority over the animal kingdom.

Bible stories also show that humans are superior beings because they are capable of having a personal relationship with their creator in a way animals cannot. What Christians believe singles humans out most of all is that they possess a soul, which animals do not. Without an immortal soul, Christians believe animals do not go to heaven.

> **Genesis 1:26a, 28**
>
> *Let us make man in our image, in our likeness, and let them… be fruitful and increase in number; fill the earth and subdue it. Rule over the fish of the sea and the birds of the air and over every living creature that moves on the ground.*

How should Christians treat animals?

Christians with more traditional views believe the Bible teaches them that animals are there to be used by people. This includes eating them, making them work for us or using them exactly as we like. They argue that animals are inferior beings and do not have the same feelings as us. In the natural world, animals prey on each other to survive.

Most Christians accept that animals can be used to improve the life of humans because it is clear that God put them on earth for our use. However, many Christians believe that whatever we do to animals should be carried out in a humane manner without causing unnecessary suffering. Because animals are part of God's creation, Christians believe it is wrong to abuse them. Some believe Jesus' message of love and compassion should be extended to our treatment of animals. Indeed Jesus said God showed concern for all his creation.

> **Luke 12:6**
>
> *Are not five sparrows sold for two pennies? Yet not one of them is forgotten by God.*

Christians are divided about whether it is acceptable to use animals for entertainment, or sport, or to make luxury items like fur coats. Many Christians agree that animals can be used for medical research because humanity benefits, but not all agree with their use in experiments for cosmetic research.

Do animals have rights?

Most Christians would say no to this. The Catholic Church says animals do not have rights but people have duties towards them because they are part of God's creation.

The Church of England says that 'the value of animals has always been seen as secondary to that of human beings, who are made in God's image and placed in a central position in creation' (*Moral Issues* 77).

Some liberal Christians believe that animals do have rights although these may not be the same rights that humans have. This is because animals are part of God's creation and DNA evidence shows humans and animals to be closely related.

Care of all God's creation

Christians believe they have a duty to care for all God's creation and this duty is called **stewardship.** Being responsible for all God's creation automatically means that Christians should care for animals. Some Christians regard the welfare of animals as part of their religious duty and give time or money to support animal charities like the RSPCA or Dogs Trust.

RESEARCH NOTE

Use the BBC news website to find out how the law relating to fox-hunting was changed. How do you think a Christian would react to fox-hunting? Why?

FOR DEBATE

Roman Catholics say animals do not have rights but people have duties towards them. What is the difference? Do you agree? What five duties might people have towards animals in their care?

ACTIVITIES

'All animals must be treated with the same respect as humans.' Do you agree with this statement? Give reasons for your answer. Explain how a Christian might respond.

Responses to environmental issues

The next two pages will help you to:

- examine Christian responses to environmental issues
- explain the concept of stewardship
- evaluate religious teachings relating to environmental issues.

Christians marching to protest against climate change.

AO1 skills ACTIVITIES

In pairs draw up your list of the ten most serious threats to the planet. Share your list with the class and jointly decide on the top ten environmental concerns of the 21st century.

How do Christians respond to the environment?

Today there is a much greater awareness of the environment and the damage that human activity is having on the planet. The world's population is larger than it has ever been and continues to grow at an ever increasing rate. This puts a strain on natural resources. At the same time our lifestyles have become more sophisticated and they not only exploit natural resources but result in greater **pollution** of the environment.

In the past, everybody lead simpler lives and did not have to concern themselves about their impact on the planet. During the 20th century and into the 21st century the situation has changed. The media keep people informed of the damage humans are doing to the planet and almost everyone has become more environmentally aware. It is normal to see recycling bins in towns, for supermarkets to ration the use of polythene carrier bags and for homes to be fitted with low-energy light bulbs.

RESEARCH NOTE

Look at the website of either A ROCHA, a Christian conservation organisation, or Christian Ecology Link. Report to the class about a project one of these groups are working on and the reasons they give for their care of the environment.

Christian stewardship

Christians all share the same environmental concerns as non-religious people but in addition they believe that God has given them a duty of **stewardship** towards the planet. The Bible says the real owner of the planet is God, not humanity.

Christians are taught that God gives the earth and all its resources to people to use in their lifetime but this must be returned to its rightful owner at the end. Christians have a duty to hand the earth back to God in the same condition they were given it. Stewardship permits people to use the earth's **natural resources** for their needs but not to destroy the environment. This means, for instance, trees that are cut down have to be replaced, fishing must never devastate the oceans' fish stocks and the land must not be poisoned by chemicals.

What are Christians taught about environmental issues?

Biblical stories about Adam and Eve in the Garden of Eden show Christians that God created a perfect environment for the first humans to live in. Not only that, God directed them to care for that environment.

When Adam and Eve disobeyed God, they were thrown out of paradise and could no longer enjoy the garden. For some Christians this is a warning about what will happen if we abuse the environment; God's created world will no longer be there for us to enjoy.

The different Christian Churches have their own teachings about environmental issues but stewardship is at the heart of them all. Compare the approach of the Orthodox Church with that of the Roman Catholic Church to environmental issues.

The Orthodox Church says:

❝ *... Just as a shepherd will in times of greatest hazard lay down his life for his flock, so human beings may need to forgo part of their wants and needs in order that the survival of the natural world can be assured. This is a new situation – a new challenge.* ❞

The Roman Catholic Church says:

❝ *A way of life that disregards and damages God's creation, forces the poor into greater poverty, and threatens the right of future generations to a healthy environment and to their fair share of the earth's wealth and resources, is contrary to the visions of the Gospel.* ❞

(*The Call of Creation*, 2002)

The Quakers say:

❝ *We do not own the world, and its riches are not ours to dispose of at will. Show a loving consideration for all creatures, and seek to maintain the beauty and variety of the world. Work to ensure that our increasing power over nature is used responsibly, with reverence for life.* ❞

(Quaker Faith & Practice 1.02.42)

Psalm 24:1

The earth is the Lord's, and everything in it, the world, and all who live in it.

 FOR DEBATE

'We will never make any progress in life if we spend all our time conserving the planet.' What are your views on this? What might Christians have to say about this?

Genesis 2:15

The Lord God took the man and put him in the Garden of Eden to work it and take care of it.

 **ACTIVITIES**

Script, or role-play, a television chat show with a celebrity interviewer who has an extravagant lifestyle and her guest who is an outspoken Christian environmentalist. Make sure there is a lively exchange of views!

Remember and Reflect

The questions in this section are based on the work you have done throughout this topic. Try to complete as many questions as you can.

The questions in set 1 are designed to test your factual recall and AO1 level skills (knowledge and understanding). The page numbers alongside the questions will help you to find information that might be useful for your answers. Use them to check against what you have written.

The questions in set 2 are more challenging, using AO2 level skills (use of evidence and reasoned argument to evaluate personal responses and differing viewpoints). Your answers many come from more than one part of the topic.

AO1 Describe, explain and analyse, using knowledge and understanding

Find the answer on:

1 Explain, in one sentence, what each of these words means.   **PAGE 45, 51**
   a *Creationist*
   b *evolution*
   c *Intelligent Design*
   d *stewardship*
   e *Darwinism*
   f *natural selection*
   g *pollution*
   h *Big Bang theory*
   i *environmental issues*

2 What is the Big Bang theory?   **PAGE 48**

3 Explain why Christians believe humans are superior to animals.   **PAGE 50**

4 What do Creationists believe about the origin of the world?   **PAGE 47–48**

5 Explain why some Christians have no problem accepting Darwinism.   **PAGE 48**

6 Give four ways in which a Christian could put stewardship into action.   **PAGE 52–53**

7 Why do some Christians reject the Creationist argument?   **PAGE 47**

8 Explain why some Christians do not think it is necessary to show special consideration to animals.   **PAGE 51**

9 Why do some Christians treat animals with great respect?   **PAGE 51**

10 Explain who Christians think really owns the planet and what difference that makes to them.   **PAGE 53**

11 Give two different Christian interpretations of the Adam and Eve story.   **PAGE 47**

12 What is meant by evolution and why would some Christians reject this idea?   **PAGE 49**

13 What evidence would some Christians give for evolution?   **PAGE 49**

AO2 Use evidence and reasoned argument to express and evaluate personal responses, informed insights, and differing viewpoints

1 Some people argue that God gave us the world so we should be free to use that present as we like. What do you think? Would all Christians agree with you?

2 In December 2008, Pope Benedict said that homosexuality posed a greater threat to the planet than climate change. What do you think?

3 Make a poster showing the different Christian responses to the origin of the world including what you think are the strengths and weakness of each argument.

4 Some people say that the stories in the Bible are only myths. How would Christians respond to that? What is your opinion?

5 Vivisection (animal experiments without the use of anaesthetic) on apes is banned in Europe but still goes on in Japan and the US. Would you agree with it given they share 99 per cent of human DNA?

6 Create a spider diagram with *God the Creator* written in the centre. Use the legs to explain the different things this can mean for Christians.

Welcome to the Grade Studio

Grade Studio is here to help you improve your grades by working through typical questions you might find on an examination paper. For a full explanation of how this feature works and how exam questions are structured, see page 14. For a full explanation of Assessment Objectives and Levels of Response, see pages x–xi in the Introduction.

AO1

Question

Explain why Christians might want to take care of the environment.   **[6 marks]**

Student's answer

Most Christians think it is important to look after the environment because it is God's world and it needs to be taken care of.

Christians might want to take care of the environment because they want everyone to have an equal chance to have a good life. They believe Jesus taught them to care for other people when he said they should love their neighbour. This includes future generations and Christians can do this by taking care of the environment.

Examiner's comment

The candidate has given a satisfactory answer to the question. There are two points stated and a third which has a brief but valid explanation, referring to the teaching of Jesus. In order to reach Level 3 the candidate needs to give more information and examples. The candidate could also use more technical terms from the specification to show the breadth of their knowledge and understanding.

Student's improved answer

Most Christians think it is important to look after the environment because it is God's world and it needs to be taken care of. Christians might want to take care of the environment because they want everyone to have an equal chance to have a good life. Jesus taught that everyone is a child of God and should be cared for. Jesus told his followers to love their neighbour, and in the Parable of the Good Samaritan he made it clear that everyone, even future generations, are a neighbour to a Christian. Environmental damage means that people will suffer and Christians should do everything to prevent and relieve suffering. Caring for the environment is a very important part of this. Christians must look after the environment so that all people have a safe world to live in and have the same chances. Christians also believe God made the world and put people in charge as stewards to look after it. The story of creation in Genesis makes this clear. Christians will put this stewardship into practice by caring for the environment.

Examiner's comment

This is now a good answer to the question. The candidate has shown a clear understanding of the question. There is good description and explanation of Christian views towards the care of the environment. The candidate has shown some analysis in in recognising the link between caring for the environment and caring for all people. The information is presented clearly and there is good use of technical terms.

AO2

Question

'If science is right about the origins of the world, religion must be wrong.' Discuss this statement. You should include different, supported points of view and a personal viewpoint. You must refer to Christianity in your answer. **[12 marks]**

Student's answer

Religion and science do not agree and so one of them must be wrong. Science is about facts which have been proved to be true like evolution, but religions are old and out of date.

Religion is also about beliefs and usually these are based on things that happened a very long time ago. For example people believe Jesus was God because he performed miracles but this cannot be proved. On the other hand, scientific experiments can prove things to be absolutely true, for example that the world revolves around the sun.

Examiner's comment

The candidate has given a limited answer to the question. There are two relevant points but the first is a matter of opinion and the other makes an assumption that because something happened a long time ago, it can't be investigated and found to be true. In order to reach Level 4 the candidate needs to give alternative viewpoints and also include a personal response.

Student's improved answer

Religion and science do not agree and so one of them must be wrong. Science is about facts which have been proved to be true like evolution, but religions are old and out of date. Religion is also about beliefs and usually these are based on things that happened a very long time ago. For example people believe Jesus was God because he performed miracles but this cannot be proved. On the other hand, scientific experiments can prove things to be absolutely true, for example that the world revolves around the sun.

Examiner's comment

This is now a good answer to the question. The candidate has shown a clear understanding of the question and has presented a range of views supported by evidence and argument. The answer explains Christian views, amongst others, and includes a personal viewpoint, which is also supported.

Through the research of modern science we now know how the world began. The Big Bang theory shows that there is no need for God and the theory of evolution shows how animals evolved and were not created. This goes against the story of creation in Genesis where God created everything in 6 days, which many Christians believe literally. However, some Christians believe that the creation story was never meant to be treated as a factual account of creation. They would say that it is possible to believe in the Big Bang and evolution at the same time as believing in religion. They say that God was the force behind the Big Bang and is the power that keeps the universe going. So science and religion are not necessarily against each other, they just see things differently.

Personally, I think that because science is based on evidence and research means that it is true. There is evidence for evolution and the Big Bang but there is no evidence for the story of creation, it is just a story. Religions started when people were ignorant and did not know any science which means their stories cannot be true. Science has shown that there is no need for a God so there will always be disagreements with people who believe religion is true.

These specimen answers provide an outline of how you could construct your response. Space does not allow us to give a full response. The examiner will be looking for more detail in your actual exam responses.

Topic 5: War, peace and human rights

The Big Picture

In this Topic, you will be addressing religious beliefs and teachings about:

- Christian attitudes towards war and the Just War theory
- attitudes towards violence and pacifism and the reasons for these
- attitudes towards human rights for Christians.

You will also think about the ways in which these beliefs affect the life and outlook of Christians in today's world.

DID YOU KNOW?

- Christians are divided between those who think fighting is never right and those who believe that fighting can be justified for moral reasons.

- Wars continue to be a key part of the human experience.

- The idea of a just war has been a key part of the thinking of both religious and non-religious people for several centuries.

KEY WORDS

atomic weapon A device which uses a nuclear explosion as a weapon.

conscientious objector Someone who refuses to fight in a war on the basis of their conscience.

justice Fairness in society and the world.

Just War theory The belief that wars can be morally justified if they follow certain criteria.

New Testament Collection of 27 books forming the second section of the Christian Bible.

nuclear pacifism Belief that the use of a nuclear weapon can never be justified.

Old Testament That part of the Christian Bible which the Church shares with Judaism, comprising 39 books covering the Hebrew Canon, and in the case of certain denominations, some books of the Apocrypha.

pacifism The belief that fighting, violence and war can never be justified.

Quaker A member of the Christian denomination also known as the Religious Society of Friends.

sin An act which goes against God's will.

violence The use of physical force, with the intention to harm.

The Commonwealth War Graves Commission (CWGC) burial ground for the dead of the First World War in Ypres, Belgium.

🕐 GET STARTED

'Christian ideas about war and peace are irrelevant to today's world as they owe their origins to the Bible.' Do you agree or disagree? Give reasons.

Do a survey to find out what people think about this question and why.

Attitudes to war and violence

The next two pages will help you to:

- examine the attitudes some people have to war and violence
- understand some Christian attitudes to war
- evaluate some of the consequences of war.

Soldiers patrolling in Iraq.

What is the point of war?

What is the point of war? One famous song of the 1970s called *War*, sung by Edwin Starr, asked what war was good for and came to the conclusion that the answer was 'absolutely nothing'. When you think of the consequences that war can have on the people involved in it, it is easy to see why a person might think it can never bring any good. These include:

- **Death:** millions were killed in wars in the last century.
- **Destruction of property and land:** this makes it difficult to re-start the economy of the nation after fighting.
- **Disease:** this often follows due to damage to food, water and medical supplies, which allows diseases like cholera to spread.
- **Mental illness:** for both the participants in the fighting and those exposed to attack, mental health issues might follow. Some soldiers might suffer from what is called post-traumatic stress disorder, where, even years later, they may have flashbacks about incidents that occurred when they were fighting.

AO1 skills ACTIVITIES

Write a list of films about, or containing, war or fighting. Why have you chosen the stories you have? Do they show war as having a point or being always wrong? Share you ideas with another couple and then present your ideas to the class so that they can then form the basis of a mind map to be put into your notes.

Attitudes to war

Some people say that despite the possible consequences, war may be an important way of dealing with situations. They believe that as human beings are naturally aggressive, war is only the predictable outcome of the way in which we have always acted. The cavemen had axes and spears, not just to kill animals for food, but to defend themselves from attack.

Some scientists think that the aggression that ends up in war has its roots in the animal origins of humanity, that it is connected with what Charles Darwin called the 'survival of the fittest'. We as one species amongst many have a desire to protect our own family or group from attack.

What are the attitudes of Christians to war?

Some Christians believe that war is often the result of sin, the evil choices people make in direct contradiction to the will of God. However, some think that, on occasion, it may still be necessary to fight in order to deal with a greater evil. Many Christians believe that war can only be fought if certain moral principles are followed.

> **St Thomas Aquinas – Summa Theologiae**
>
> *For a war to be just, three conditions are necessary – public authority, just cause, right motive.*

Many Christians believe that the rejection of war and violence is what Jesus stressed in the gospels. They believe in **pacifism** – the belief that peace should be the central value people pursue; this will normally mean that violence and war are seen as unacceptable. They quote such sayings of Jesus as:

> **Matthew 26:52a**
>
> *For all who draw the sword will die by the sword.*

They may say that no Christian believed in fighting for the government or in war until the Romans officially adopted Christianity and it became the religion of the Empire.

Attitudes to war continue to develop amongst Christians, especially as they reflect on the way in which modern technology can influence the way a war is waged.

RESEARCH NOTE

Using the Internet, research in detail a war in the news or one you would like to understand more about. Find out the causes of the war, the consequences and the differing views people had about the need to fight or not. Prepare a PowerPoint presentation for the class.

AO2 skills **ACTIVITIES**

'The consequences of war are always so negative that there can be no good reasons for going to war.' What do you think of this statement? What might a Christian say? Give reasons for your answers, showing that you have though about it from more than one point of view.

How does the Bible influence Christians about war, peace and justice?

The next two pages will help you to:

- consider the use of the Bible as a source for Christian teaching and belief about war
- explore how the Bible is sometimes used to justify or condemn war
- evaluate the effects the Bible has on Christian behaviour regarding war, peace and justice.

AO1 skills ACTIVITIES

'The Bible is a book of peace.' What do you think of this statement?

The death of the Egyptians in the Red Sea from a 10th-century Bible.

What does the Old Testament teach about war and peace?

The Bible is a collection of 66 books which were written over the space of a thousand years. These were collected into one volume and have come to be seen as special, as revealed by God through their writers to lead Christians and others into the truths about God. The Bible is seen as an authority, as God revealed Himself in its word. It can be used as a guide to life, especially on issues such as war, peace and justice. It is divided into two parts, the **Old Testament** and the **New Testament**. The Old Testament contains writings that are considered sacred to the Jews.

The world of the Old Testament is often seen as bloody and warlike. The years it deals with saw empires like those of the Egyptians, Assyrians, Babylonians, Persians, Greeks and Romans rise and fall.

In the book of Exodus 15:3, there is a song that celebrates the defeat of the Egyptians – 'The Lord is a warrior; the Lord is his name'. For many people, the idea of God as a warrior is problematic. How could he fight on one side or the other?

The vision of peace in the book of Micah

The prophet Micah had a vision of a peaceful world in Micah Chapter 4:1–4. He is looking beyond warfare and conflict to a time of universal peace. Read verse 3 from that passage in the box opposite. What teachings are in this verse?

> **Micah 4:1–4**
>
> *He will judge between many peoples*
> *and will settle disputes for strong nations far and wide.*
> *They will beat their swords into ploughshares*
> *and their spears into pruning hooks.*
> *Nation will not take up sword against nation,*
> *nor will they train for war anymore.*

What does the New Testament teach about war and peace?

Look at the sacred texts opposite. What do you think these passages mean? Some Christians believe that passages such as the ones above mean that it can never be right to fight in a war as Jesus' teachings will not be followed if people fight.

Other Christians argue that these passages are only about an individual who is a Christian; they cannot or should not be taken to apply to whole nations or to the need to defend your country if it is threatened.

Look at this account of the arrest of Jesus from Matthew 26:47–52. Look what Jesus says at this arrest 'Put your sword back in its place ... for all who draw the sword will die by the sword.'

Many Christians see the non-violent way in which Jesus responded to his arrest and his time on the Cross as an example of how people should behave. If he did not choose **violence** at this time, then how can they? Jesus points to the destructive nature of violence. However, when Jesus saw the money-lenders in the Temple he became very angry and threw them out.

The Christian leader St Paul wrote:

> **Matthew 5:43–44**
>
> *You have heard that it was said, 'Love your neighbour and hate your enemy.' But I tell you: Love your enemies and pray for those who persecute you.*

> **Matthew 5:9**
>
> *Blessed are the peacemakers, for they will be called sons of God.*

> **Romans 12:17–21**
>
> *Do not repay anyone evil for evil. Be careful to do what is right in the eyes of everybody. If it is possible, as far as it depends on you, live at peace with everyone. Do not take revenge, my friends, but leave room for God's wrath, for it is written: "It is mine to avenge; I will repay," says the Lord. On the contrary: "If your enemy is hungry, feed him; if he is thirsty, give him something to drink. In doing this, you will heap burning coals on his head." Do not be overcome by evil, but overcome evil with good.*

Many Christians believe that you should not try to overcome evil with force as in a war. Others disagree and say that in exceptional circumstances, force may be necessary in order to achieve a just world.

AO2 skills ACTIVITIES

'When you read the New Testament, you cannot come to the conclusion that fighting is right.' What do you think? What would a Christian say? Show that you have thought about your answer from several different points of view.

What do Christians believe about a just war, pacifism and violence?

What is meant by the Just War theory?

Some people feel that the only justification for war would be if they were defending, either their own country or another country. Britain went to war against Germany in 1939 as they were seeking to defend Poland against being invaded.

Some wars might need to be fought, so how could they be seen as morally necessary? In a book called the *Summa Theologiae*, the Christian thinker St Thomas Aquinas (1225–74), wrote about a theory of **just war**, a war that it is better to fight than not. Some of these principles preceded Aquinas and others were developed later. To be a just war, the war must follow certain criteria. Here are six that are very important:

1   The war must be fought for a just cause. There must be a just or moral reason, such as defending a nation under attack or trying to stop a tyranny.

2   There must only be controlled **violence**. Every effort must be made to make sure that as little violence is used as possible. Any use of force that is more than the enemy can or has used is seen as immoral.

3   A war can be fought if it is believed that a greater evil would exist if the war were not fought. People argue that if Britain and her allies had not taken on the Nazi regime of Adolf Hitler, then far greater evil would have happened.

4   In order for a war to be just, it must be in the control of the politicians and not just dominated by the military in the war zone. They can take only minor decisions, the politicians should be able to take the most important.

5   The force used in the war should be proportional. **Proportionality** means that the amount of force should not be excessive. The military should also try to avoid injuring innocent civilians.

6   Only the military should be involved in the fighting of the war and they should seek to avoid the damage of property and others.

What is pacifism?

Pacifism is the belief that the use of violence to fight in a war or to defend yourself is not right. For many Christians, this is rooted in their belief that Jesus taught people to be non-violent. For the first three centuries CE, Christians did not serve in armies or fight in wars.

AO1 skills **ACTIVITIES**

What do you think are good reasons for war? Try to list as many of these as you can. Share your lists with a partner and then as a class.

 **FOR DEBATE**

Can the ideas of the Just War theory still work in the world we live in?

However, when the Emperor Constantine made Christianity the state religion, the Roman Empire began to convince Christians that they had to fight in order to protect their faith. For example, he and subsequent leaders of Christian countries have put the Cross on their shields or provided priests to support the troops and bring a spiritual dimension to the fighting. Down the centuries, the Christian church has often argued for Just War theory, though there are many people to this day who campaign for non-violent resistance.

Some Christians have made a distinction between pacifism and what they call **nuclear pacifism**. A nuclear pacifist believes that the use of an **atomic weapon** can never be justified as the consequences of the use of such a weapon would never be equal to the evil that needed to be defeated. They do not necessarily rule out the use of force in other ways.

What is the Quaker approach to war?

The Religious Society of Friends, or **Quakers** as they are also known, have been committed to pacifism from their origins. They believe that this is what Jesus required. One of the famous statements of their principles is called the Quaker Peace Testimony (below). It was written at a time when the king, Charles II, accused them of being involved in plots against his reign:

Quaker Peace Testimony

We utterly deny all outward wars and strife and fighting with outward weapons for any end or under any pretense whatsoever; this is our testimony to the whole world... The Spirit of Christ by which we are guided is not changeable, so as once to command us from a thing of evil and again to move us into it; and we certainly know and testify to the world that the Spirit of Christ which leads us into all truth will never move us to fight and war against any man with outward weapons, neither for the Kingdom of Christ nor for the kingdoms of this world... therefore we cannot learn war anymore.

To this day, Quakers are conscientious objectors – that is they refuse to fight in wars. However, they may be involved in the medical care needed for those caught up in conflict.

Attitudes to violence

Some Christians believe that pacifism is not just about the issue of war but that such an attitude should characterise any violence, feeling that Jesus' teaching was clearly about non-violence. Others believe that the use of force to restrain is acceptable, but that if it leads to violence that can wound, then it is not.

Many Christians extend these beliefs about violence to all aspects of their life. They do not believe that violence can ever be justified. However, others may say that when Jesus threw the money-lenders out of the Temple in Jerusalem (Matthew 21:10–17) he was acting in a violent manner and that sometimes violence may be justified.

ACTIVITIES

'The Just War theory is irrelevant to the 21st century.' What do you think of this statement? What might Christians say? Show that you have thought about it from several points of view.

Human rights

The next two pages will help you to:

- explain what Christians believe about human rights and prisoners of conscience
- evaluate the way in which Christian teachings have helped develop views on justice.

Amnesty International campaigns for human rights across the world.

What is the Universal Declaration of Human Rights?

When the United Nations was set up just after the Second World War, the countries that formed the organisation all agreed to a set of principles called the Universal Declaration of Human Rights. There are thirty parts of this but here are some examples:

- **Article 1:** All human beings are born free and equal in dignity and rights. They are endowed with reason and conscience and should act towards one another in a spirit of brotherhood.
- **Article 3:** Everyone has the right to life, liberty and security of person.
- **Article 4:** No one shall be held in slavery or servitude; slavery and the slave trade shall be prohibited in all their forms.
- **Article 5:** No one shall be subjected to torture or to cruel, inhuman or degrading treatment or punishment.

Although the Universal Declaration of Human Rights does not include any specifically Christian teachings, it is based on humanitarian principles, many of which reflect the teachings of the Bible.

Some people who are arrested for their non-violent beliefs are called prisoners of conscience and organisations like Amnesty International campaign for their release.

A prisoner of conscience is anyone who is imprisoned because of their race, religion, colour, language, gender, sexual orientation, belief or lifestyle as long as they have not used **violence** or promoted its use.

ACTIVITIES

Write down the phrase 'It's not fair when…' and add five endings to it in relation to human rights. For example: 'It's not fair when a person is treated differently because of the colour of their skin.' Compare your five sentences with the person sitting next to you. What do your answers have in common? What is different? What is personal? What is about the world or society in general?

RESEARCH NOTE

Go to the United Nations website, and look up the remaining parts of the Universal Declaration of Human Rights. Are there rights that it does not cover which you think are important?

How do Christian teachings help a believer develop their views on justice?

The world often lacks **justice** and people are not treated fairly. There are many ways in which humans are divided from each other and these are often used as reasons to be unfair; for example, differences in race, religion, sex, sexuality, wealth or class. Many Christians would say that one of the reasons for this is that humans have sinned; they have rebelled against God and caused evil to come into existence.

Many Christians turn to the Bible to find inspiration for their work in helping with human rights. Christians believe that God created all people. In Genesis 1:27 it says, 'So God created man in his own image, in the image of God he created him; male and female he created them.' This suggests that all people are important to God: they are in his image in that they are loving, spiritual beings and are therefore entitled to dignity. For many Christians, this is an important passage when considering the idea of human rights.

The **Old Testament** is full of the words of prophets calling for justice, such as the prophet Isaiah in this passage from Chapter 58 verses 6 to 7:

> *Is not this the kind of fasting I have chosen:*
> *to loose the chains of injustice*
> *and untie the cords of the yoke,*
> *to set the oppressed free*
> *and break every yoke?*
> *Is it not to share your food with the hungry*
> *and to provide the poor wanderer with shelter –*
> *when you see the naked, to clothe him,*
> *and not to turn away from your own flesh and blood?*

This teaching makes very clear that God requires his followers to practise justice and care for people less fortunate then themselves.

For Christians, reading prophecies like this and thinking about the life and teachings of Jesus can inspire them to be involved in trying to make the world a better, more just society, committed to human rights.

AO2 skills ACTIVITIES

'A just world is impossible and therefore we should not even attempt to get one.' What do you think? What might Christians say? Refer in detail to Christian teachings to make your case.

The questions in this section are based on the work you have done throughout this topic. Try to complete as many questions as you can.

The questions in set 1 are designed to test your factual recall and AO1 level skills (knowledge and understanding). The page numbers alongside the questions will help you to find information that might be useful for your answers. Use them to check against what you have written.

The questions in set 2 are more challenging, using AO2 level skills (use of evidence and reasoned argument to evaluate personal responses and differing viewpoints). Your answers many come from more than one part of the topic.

AO1 Describe, explain and analyse, using knowledge and understanding

Find the answer on:

1 Explain, in one sentence, what each of the following key words means:
   a Just War
   b pacifism
   c proportionality
   d nuclear pacifism

   PAGE 58, 64

2 Why is the Bible important to Christians in making decisions about war?

   PAGE 62

3 Explain some of the consequences of war.

   PAGE 60

4 Explain some of the causes of war.

   PAGE 62–63

5 Why do Christians believe the Old Testament is important in helping them develop their views about war?

   PAGE 64

6 Explain, giving examples, some of the teachings about war in the Old Testament.

   PAGE 62–63

7 Explain, giving examples, the teachings you will find in the New Testament about war.

   PAGE 63

8 Explain what Christians mean by 'being in the image of God'.

   PAGE 67

9 Give three reasons why a Christian might be a pacifist.

   PAGE 65

10 Outline three ways in which Christians use the Bible to justify their support for a war.

   PAGE 64

11 Explain the Universal Declaration of Human Rights.

   PAGE 66

12 Give three examples of human rights.

   PAGE 66–67

13 Write down three arguments that Christians might use to back the idea of human rights.

   PAGE 67

14 Outline three reasons for a war to be declared just.

   PAGE 64

AO2 Use evidence and reasoned argument to express and evaluate personal responses, informed insights, and differing viewpoints

1   Answer the following, giving as much detail as possible. You should give at least three reasons to support your response and also show that you have taken into account opposite opinions.
   a   *Considering the teaching of the New Testament, Christians should not support the idea of a just war.*
   b   *Do you think Christian teaching contained in the Bible is relevant to the wars of today's world?*
   c   *Considering the sin in people's lives do you feel that pacifism is unrealistic?*
   d   *What would you say are the essential things a Christian should believe about war?*

2   'There can never be agreement between Christians about war.' Do you agree? What might Christians think? Show that you have thought about several points of view in your answer.

3   'Nuclear pacifism is not workable.' Do you agree? What might Christians think? Show that you have thought about several points of view in your answer.

4   'Human rights are nothing to do with religious opinions.' Do you agree? What might Christians think? Show that you have thought about several points of view in your answer.

5   'The world will never be fair.' What might a Christian think about this? What could be done to try to improve it?

6   'Christians should spend their time preparing themselves for heaven, not bothering about the world of here and now.' Do you agree?

Welcome to the Grade Studio

Grade Studio is here to help you improve your grades by working through typical questions you might find on an examination paper. For a full explanation of how this feature works and how exam questions are structured, see page 14. For a full explanation of Assessment Objectives and Levels of Response, see pages x–xi in the Introduction.

AO1

Question

What are Christian attitudes towards war?   [6 marks]

Student's answer

Christians are pacifists and believe that all war is wrong because Jesus was a pacifist.

Some Christians believe that there are occasions such as a 'Just War' which meet certain conditions and when it is right to fight in order to protect people. An example could be self defence.

Examiner's comment

The candidate has given a satisfactory answer to the question. There are two main points but only one of them, about 'Just War', has any valid explanation, but that is brief and does not add much to the answer. In order to reach Level 3 the candidate needs to give more information and examples. The candidate could also use more technical terms from the specification to show the breadth of their knowledge and understanding.

Student's improved answer

Christians are pacifists and believe that all war is wrong because Jesus was a pacifist.

Some Christians believe that there are occasions such as a 'Just War' which meet certain conditions and when it is right to fight in order to protect people or in self defence. Another could be that it is right to fight as long as civilians are not harmed.

Some Christians say that there are examples in the Bible of wars that were fought with God's approval and help. Some Christians have beleievd it is right to fight in a Holy War, which is fought to protect the Christian religion. However there are some Christians such as Quakers (The Religious Society of Friends) who are total pacifists and will not fight under any circumstances. They follow Jesus' teaching of turning the other cheek rather then fighting back.

Examiner's comment

This is now a good answer to the question. The candidate has shown a clear understanding of the question. There is good description and explanation of a variety of different attitudes towards war. The candidate has shown some analysis in dealing with the Quakers. The information is presented clearly and there is good use of technical terms.

Question

'All people must be pacifists.' Discuss this statement. You should include different, supported points of view and a personal viewpoint. You must refer to Christianity in your answer. **[12 marks]**

Student's answer

Some Christians say that all people must be pacifists because they believe that Jesus was a pacifist and never hurt anybody. Other Christians believe that the commandment says 'do not kill' and that therefore any fighting must be wrong because people risk being killed. Jesus told people to turn the other cheek when they were hit and not to seek revenge, so even fighting in self defence is wrong. Two wrongs don't make a right.

Examiner's comment

The candidate has given a limited answer to the question. There are two relevant points but one is a matter of opinion and the other is a common misinterpretation resulting in a misunderstanding. In order to reach Level 4 the candidate needs to give alternative viewpoints and also include a personal response.

Student's improved answer

Some Christians say that all people must be pacifists because they believe that Jesus was a pacifist and never hurt anybody. Other Christians believe that the commandment says 'do not kill' and that therefore any fighting must be wrong because people risk being killed. Jesus told people to turn the other cheek when they were hit and not to seek revenge, so even fighting in self defence is wrong. Two wrongs don't make a right.

Some people, on the other hand, might think that there are circumstances, such as during a 'Just War', when it is necessary for Christians and others to fight. To do nothing would be wrong and would let evil win. Christian thinkers have devised some rules for a war which is just or right such as self defence, ensuring civilians are not hurt, only using a reasonable amount of force and making sure the war will produce a better situation than existed before the conflict. My personal opinion is that it is not easy to decide whether to be a total pacifist.

There may be circumstances, such as during the Second World War, where people have a duty to fight in order to protect their country from being overrun by evil. I could not stand by and let my family be killed I would have to do something to stop it which would mean I had to fight. So I think it would be great if all people were pacifists because there would be peace everywhere, but as they are not, it will sometimes be necessary to fight which is the less evil thing to do than allow evil to win.

Examiner's comment

This is now a good answer to the question. The candidate has shown a clear understanding of the question and has presented a range of views supported by evidence and argument. The answer explains Christian views, amongst others, and includes a personal viewpoint, which is also supported.

These specimen answers provide an outline of how you could construct your response. Space does not allow us to give a full response. The examiner will be looking for more detail in your actual exam responses.

Topic 6: Prejudice and equality

The Big Picture

In this Topic, you will be addressing Christian beliefs and teachings about:

- the principle of equality
- attitudes towards racism
- attitudes towards gender
- attitudes towards other religions.

You will also think about the ways in which these beliefs affect the life and outlook of Christians in today's world.

DID YOU KNOW?

- Some Christians say that the Bible teaches that everyone is equal in the sight of God.

- Most Christians believe that racial discrimination is always wrong. Many Christians devote their lives to fighting racism and other discrimination.

- Some Christians believe that God created men and women to have different roles; others think that they should have the right to choose. Some believe that only men should become priests, but there are now many women priests and ministers. Members of the Church of England disagree about whether women should be allowed to become bishops.

- Some Christians think Christianity is the only true religion and that all other religions are false. Many Christians are committed to evangelism, while others work to develop interfaith understanding. Some Christians support the ecumenical movement, helping Christians of different denominations to understand each other better.

'Women are still not paid as much as men.' Are you surprised that this is still the case in modern society? What do you think are the reasons for this? Is this unfair?

There is now greater equality between men and women in work.

KEY WORDS

Crusade Religiously sanctioned war, often about the control of a sacred place.

discrimination Unjust or prejudicial treatment because of race, age, gender or disability.

ecumenical Different Christian denominations working together.

equality Treating people as equals regardless of gender, race or religious beliefs.

Evangelism Persuading others to share your faith.

prejudice Making judgements not based on reason or actual experience.

proselytising Trying to convert people from their religion to yours.

racism Prejudice, discrimination or ill treatment against someone because of their race.

sexism Prejudice, stereotyping or discrimination, typically against women, on the basis of sex.

What is equality?

Equality

The next two pages will help you to:

- examine the principle of equality
- examine Biblical teachings about equality
- evaluate Christian attitudes towards equality.

The two words which are frequently used when talking about **equality** are **prejudice** and **discrimination**.

- **Prejudice:** an idea or feeling which one person holds and which affects another person.
- **Discrimination:** action based on prejudice.

On 10 December 1948 the General Assembly of the United Nations formally adopted the United Nations Declaration of Human Rights (see 5.4). The first two articles state that everyone in the world should have exactly the same rights and freedoms:

- **Article 1:** All human beings are born free and equal in dignity and rights. They are endowed with reason and conscience and should act towards one another in a spirit of brotherhood.
- **Article 2:** Everyone is entitled to all the rights and freedoms set forth in this Declaration, without distinction of any kind, such as race, colour, sex, language, religion, political or other opinion, national or social origin, property, birth or other status.

Despite the Declaration, the media shows every day that thousands of people suffer from inequality and discrimination.

Eleanor Roosevelt (1884–1962) was the first chairperson of the UN Human Rights commission which produced the Declaration of Human Rights.

What does the Bible teach about equality?

Christians are told that all humans are made 'in the image of God' (Genesis 1:27). They believe that all humans matter to God, regardless of race, gender, ability, wealth or skills, and that all who pray to God will be listened to and treated without favouritism. As a result of God's attitude to humans, they should treat others with the same respect.

Christians also believe that they should treat others in the way they would wish to be treated: 'Love your neighbour as yourself' (Luke 10:27b).

AO1 skills ACTIVITIES

Keep a list for a day. On your list make two columns, one of things which happen that you think are fair and one of things which you think are unfair. Compare your list with a partner. Which events do you disagree on?

 MUST THINK ABOUT!

Some people say that discrimination = prejudice + power.

Christian attitudes towards equality

When it comes to specific teaching on equality there are passages in both the Old and New Testaments of the Bible:

Leviticus 19:33–34

When an alien lives with you in your land, do not ill-treat him. The alien living with you must be treated as one of your native-born. Love him as yourself, for you were aliens in Egypt. I am the Lord your God.

Galatians 3:28

There is neither Jew nor Greek, slave nor free, male nor female, for you are all one in Christ Jesus.

The first passage refers to the time that the Israelites were slaves in Egypt. However, although the second passage is often taken to mean that, according to Christianity, everyone is equal; some scholars believe that it simply says that all Christians are equal.

There are also teachings about not showing favouritism to particular people.

James 2:1

My brothers, as believers in our glorious Lord Jesus Christ, don't show favouritism.

Acts 10:34–35

Then Peter began to speak: 'I now realise how true it is that God does not show favouritism but accepts men from every nation who fear him and do what is right.

Christian views on prejudice and discrimination

Christians believe that they should follow the example of Jesus, therefore all people should be treated in the same way. Jesus healed the son of a Roman centurion, even though the Romans were hated; he showed respect for women, who were generally seen as less important than men; and he made a Samaritan the hero of one of his most famous parables, even though the people of Samaria were not respected by the Jews.

The parable of The Good Samaritan

Luke 10:30–35a

Jesus said: 'A man was going down from Jerusalem to Jericho, when he fell into the hands of robbers. They stripped him of his clothes, beat him and went away, leaving him half dead. A priest happened to be going down the same road, and when he saw the man, he passed by on the other side. So too, a Levite, when he came to the place and saw him, passed by on the other side. But a Samaritan, as he travelled, came where the man was; and when he saw him, he took pity on him. He went to him and bandaged his wounds, pouring on oil and wine. Then he put the man on his own donkey, took him to an inn and took care of him. The next day he took out two silver coins and gave them to the innkeeper. 'Look after him,' he said.

RESEARCH NOTE

Find a copy of the United Nations Declaration of Human Rights on the Internet. Read the preamble and then explain, in your own words, why the Declaration was written.

FOR DEBATE

'All animals are born equal, but some are more equal than others.' Discuss what this quotation from George Orwell's book *Animal Farm* means. Decide whether you agree with it and explain your opinions.

AO2 skills ACTIVITIES

'Not everyone is equal.' Do you agree? How might a Christian respond to this statement?

Discrimination because of colour and race

Christianity and racism

There have been many occasions in the history of Christianity when the behaviour of individuals or groups of Christians would be described as racist. During the **Crusades** thousands of people across Europe and the Middle East were killed in the name of Christianity.

During their voyages of exploration in the 16th century, Spain invaded South America. Tens of thousands of the inhabitants were killed in attempts to force them to convert to Christianity. At the same time the Spanish navy took all their wealth. The slave plantations of the Caribbean and the American Deep South were mostly owned by Christians.

Slavery was abolished in the United States of America at the end of the Civil War in 1865. The southern states of America were forced to accept the 13th amendment:

66 *Neither slavery nor involuntary servitude, except as a punishment for crime whereof the party shall have been duly convicted, shall exist within the United States, or any place subject to their jurisdiction.* **99**

There are some passages in the New Testament which have been used to support slavery.

This memorial in Soweto, South Africa, honours the memory of Hector Pieterson (1964–76) who was killed during student riots against the apartheid regime.

1 Corinthians 7:21–22

Were you a slave when called? Do not be concerned about it. Even if you can gain your freedom, make use of your present condition now more than ever. For whoever was called in the Lord as a slave is a freed person belonging to the Lord, just as whoever was free when called is a slave of Christ.

However, the Christian Church today condemns any form of slavery. In 1948, in South Africa, the Prime Minister, the Reverend Daniel François Malan, introduced the legislation known as apartheid. Under these laws people were separated by their skin colour: black, white or coloured. This was supported by the Dutch Reformed Church of which Malan was a minister.

AO1 skills ACTIVITIES

In pairs, write down as many different types of discrimination as you can think of. Remember, sometimes discrimination can be a good thing. Share your list with a group and then with the whole class. How many different types did you think of? How many of these types are positive?

Apartheid was condemned by the World Alliance of Reformed Churches in the 1980s and the Dutch Reformed Church was expelled from the Alliance. In 1986 all congregations in the church were desegregated. However, it was not until 1994 that apartheid was finally abolished in South Africa.

Dr Martin Luther King Jr (1929–68)

One of the most famous Americans of all time and the leader of the protests against racial **discrimination** was Martin Luther King Jr (1929–68). Martin Luther King Jr was a black Baptist minister and the son of a Baptist minister.

He experienced **racism** and segregation all his life and made it his life's work to try to improve the laws of the USA to prevent racism. He was also an admirer of Mahatma Gandhi and followed his principle of satyagraha (peaceful protest).

Martin Luther King Jr's most famous speech was made on 28 August 1963 on the steps of the Lincoln Memorial in Washington, DC.

❝ I have a dream that one day every valley shall be exalted, every hill and mountain shall be made low, the rough places will be made plain, and the crooked places will be made straight, and the glory of the Lord shall be revealed, and all flesh shall see it together.

This will be the day when all of God's children will be able to sing with a new meaning, 'My country, 'tis of thee, sweet land of liberty, of thee I sing. Land where my fathers died, land of the pilgrim's pride, from every mountainside, let freedom ring.'

And when this happens, When we allow freedom to ring, when we let it ring from every village and every hamlet, from every state and every city, we will be able to speed up that day when all of God's children, black men and white men, Jews and Gentiles, Protestants and Catholics, will be able to join hands and sing in the words of the old Negro spiritual, 'Free at last! free at last! thank God Almighty, we are free at last!' ❞

RESEARCH NOTE

Research the first four Crusades and produce a PowerPoint presentation about them.

Dr Martin Luther King Jr.

MUST THINK ABOUT!

Gandhi's teaching of satyagraha (non-violent protest) was based on the Hindu idea of ahimsa (non-violence). By leading non-violent protests he was able to persuade Britain to give back India its independence in 1947.

 ACTIVITIES
AO2 skills

'Christians should always fight to stop racism.' Do you agree? How might a Christian respond to this statement?

Discrimination because of gender

The next two pages will help you to:

- examine Christian views on sexism
- evaluate how Christians have responded to sexism.

Some Christian Churches allow women to be priests.

Christian views about women

Sexism is a form of **prejudice** based on gender, typically against women. In the past, many people felt that men and women possessed different skills, and this has resulted in their being treated differently.

The Church has often been accused of being sexist. The language used in the Church seems to be in favour of men and God is almost always referred to as being male.

Some Christians believe that God made men and women differently, and passages such as 'God made man in his own image' are often used against those who demand greater **equality** in the Church and society. The Hebrew original reads 'God made a human being in his own image.'

There are several passages in the New Testament where St Paul appears to be saying that women are inferior to men.

 **ACTIVITIES**

Make a list of jobs which are traditionally associated with women and another of those associated with men. Compare your list with a partner's. Look at your lists and ask each other whether there is any real reason for a job to be in one column rather than the other. If you think there is a reason then you must explain it.

> **1 Corinthians 14:34–35**
>
> *Women should remain silent in the churches. They are not allowed to speak, but must be in submission, as the Law says. If they want to enquire about something, they should ask their own husbands at home; for it is disgraceful for a woman to speak in the church.*

> **1 Corinthians 11:3**
>
> *Now I want you to realise that the head of every man is Christ, and the head of the woman is man, and the head of Christ is God.*

This has led to a traditional view that men should go out to work to provide for the family while women bring up children and run the home. However, many Christians now feel that men and women should be given equal opportunities and responsibilities in the workplace and at home.

However, it is important to remember that, according to Mark's gospel, after the resurrection Jesus first appeared to a woman:

Mark 16:9
Now after he rose early on the first day of the week, he appeared first to Mary Magdalene, from whom he had cast out seven demons.

Women in the Church

Christians believe in equality, although this may not mean that all people are able to do the same job. There is a strong feeling in some denominations that women should have no part in the Ministry of the Word of God.

The Christian church has been very slow in changing its position in relation to women. In the Roman Catholic Church, women are not accepted as priests as it is felt that only men should say the words spoken by Jesus that are repeated during the Mass. It is also thought that because God came to earth in the form of a man – Jesus – his representatives on earth should only be men and the twelve apostles chosen by Jesus were all men. St Paul also taught that women 'should be silent'.

However, many other denominations have long accepted women in their ministry. Methodists, Baptists and others allow both men and women to be ministers, to preach and to have equal responsibility. The Church of England accepted women as vicars in 1994. Some Anglicans disagree with this and have not been comfortable with women taking over their parish (the area the priest is responsible for).

In recent years many Christians have argued that that women should have an equal role in worship and the priesthood not just on grounds of equality but because of what happened in the early Church:

Acts 1:12–14
They all joined together constantly in prayer, along with the women and Mary the mother of Jesus, and with his brothers.

It also appears that woman were important in the early Church:

Romans 16:1–5
I commend to you our sister Phoebe, a servant of the church in Cenchrea. I ask you to receive her in the Lord in a way worthy of the saints and to give her any help she may need from you, for she has been a great help to many people, including me. Greet Priscilla and Aquila, my fellow workers in Christ Jesus. They risked their lives for me. Not only I but all the churches of the Gentiles are grateful to them. Greet also the church that meets at their house.

 MUST THINK ABOUT!

There are female Anglican vicars, but no female Anglican bishops as yet.

 **ACTIVITIES**

'If men and women are equal then women can become priests.' Do you agree? How might a Christian respond to this statement? Examine what this might mean for different Christian denominations.

Attitudes towards other religions

The next two pages will help you to:

- examine Christian views about other religions
- understand what is meant by missionary work and evangelism
- consider Christian work towards ecumenism.

ACTIVITIES

Visit the Church Mission Society and the BMS World Mission websites to research the work undertaken by a missionary society. Produce a leaflet to highlight the variety and scope of the activities of your chosen society.

The motto of the Church Mission Society.

Christianity and other religions

Christianity is a religion that believes in evangelism. This means that Christians believe that they should try to encourage everyone to become members of their faith. This is because of the commission Jesus gave to the disciples. There are other Christians who believe that if people are following their own religion then they are also worshipping God.

MUST THINK ABOUT!

Islam and Christianity are proselytising religions. However, some other religions such as Judaism do not encourage converts because they believe that people can serve God through a different religion.

Matthew 28:16–20a

Then the eleven disciples went to Galilee, to the mountain where Jesus had told them to go. When they saw him, they worshipped him; but some doubted. Then Jesus came to them and said, 'All authority in heaven and on earth has been given to me. Therefore go and make disciples of all nations, baptising them in the name of the Father and of the Son and of the Holy Spirit, and teaching them to obey everything I have commanded you.'

So although Christians believe that everyone should have the right to practise their own religion they also believe that only Christianity has the complete truth about God.

Missionaries

This commission to spread the gospel, or evangelise, is taken seriously by many Christians, who feel that they should become involved in missionary work – bringing the Christian message to people in their own country and all over the world. For hundreds of years Christians travelled around the world as missionaries. These people felt that, as Christians, it was their duty to convert as many people as possible. They believed that it was only by becoming Christians that people had a chance of reaching heaven when they died.

Christians involved in missionary work feel that it is essential to give everyone the opportunity to follow the Christian faith in order to know God. John's Gospel explains this: Jesus answered: 'I am the way and the truth and the life. No one comes to the Father except by me' (John 14:6). There are still missionary societies today. However, while they are still concerned with spreading the Christian message, their main purpose is to help people in developing countries by following the example of Jesus.

Ecumenism

This is the name given to the movement that tries to unite different Christians. There are hundreds of different Christian groups and often they have different ways of practising their faith. Many denominations – mostly Protestant and Orthodox – meet as members of the World Council of Churches in order to celebrate the fact that all confess the Lord Jesus Christ, according to the Holy Scriptures, as God and Saviour. The spirit of ecumenism has been encouraged by many of the Asian and African Churches, which have demonstrated great courage in the face of persecution.

Several Christian communities have been established to help members of different denominations come together to worship.

Taizé

In 1940 Roger Schutz founded a religious community of monks at Taizé in France that sheltered Jewish refugees escaping Nazi Germany until 1942. When the Nazis occupied France, Roger had to leave but returned at the end of the war, initially caring for German prisoners of war, practising the Christian belief of forgiveness and reconciliation.

Taizé is a place of pilgrimage particularly for young people from all over the world and, as an **ecumenical** community, works to break down barriers between Christian denominations.

The monks are also from different churches and different countries.

Young people camp in the fields, join in daily worship and help with practical work in the kitchens and on the farms. Worship includes simple songs in Latin, French, German and English. There is time for meditation and reflection allowing young people to develop self-awareness of what is in their heart and to listen to God. Times of group discussion encourage listening skills and provide a chance to discuss the challenges of being a young Christian.

Living a simpler monastic life without television and luxuries helps people find a meaning to life and to decide what is really important.

ACTIVITIES

'All Christians should forget their differences and worship together.' Do you agree with this statement? How might a Christian respond to this statement?

Remember and Reflect

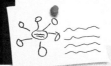

The questions in this section are based on the work you have done throughout this topic. Try to complete as many questions as you can.

The questions in set 1 are designed to test your factual recall and AO1 level skills (knowledge and understanding). The page numbers alongside the questions will help you to find information that might be useful for your answers. Use them to check against what you have written.

The questions in set 2 are more challenging, using AO2 level skills (use of evidence and reasoned argument to evaluate personal responses and differing viewpoints). Your answers many come from more than one part of the topic.

AO1 Describe, explain and analyse, using knowledge and understanding

Find the answer on:

1 What is meant by:
  a prejudice
  b discrimination
  c equality?

PAGE 73

2 Name three reasons for which people might be discriminated against.

PAGE 74

3 Explain what is meant by discrimination = power + prejudice.

PAGE 74

4 Give examples of two Biblical teachings about equality, one from the Old Testament and one from the New Testament.

PAGE 75

5 What is meant by 'proselytising' or 'evangelising'?

PAGE 73

6 Explain the traditional role of a missionary.

PAGE 81

7 Explain how missionaries work today.

PAGE 81

8 What were the Crusades?

PAGE 76

9 Why did the Spanish navy kill so many people in South America?

PAGE 76

10 What does the New Testament say about slavery?

PAGE 76

11 Explain what is meant by apartheid.

PAGE 76

12 Which Christian denomination supported apartheid?

PAGE 76

13 What is satyagraha?

PAGE 77

14 Which famous American Civil Rights leader was assassinated in 1968?

PAGE 77

AO2 Use evidence and reasoned argument to express and evaluate personal responses, informed insights, and differing viewpoints

1 'It is not possible to treat everyone equally.' Do you agree with this statement? Explain your thinking on this issue.

2 Do you think that all churches should ordain women as priests? Construct a set of arguments for and against this statement.

3 What do you think a Christian would say to the following question 'Why does the Church treat men and women differently?'

4 'The existence of black churches shows that Christianity is still racist.' Do you agree with this statement? Explain your thinking on this issue.

5 'All people are equal in the eyes of God and therefore there should be no leaders in church.' Do you agree with this statement? Explain your thinking on this issue.

6 'All responses to discrimination should be non-violent.' Construct a paragraph that a Christian might write in response to this statement.

7 'The first two articles of the United Nations' Declaration of Human Rights do not agree with Christian teaching.' Consider the arguments for and against this statement and weigh these up to come to a conclusion.

8 Copy and complete the table below to show how a Christian, a non-believer, and you would respond to the statements. (Remember: not all religious believers agree on everything, so try to reflect this in your answers.) Make sure you include references to religious knowledge and give as many reasons for each view as possible.

Statement	What would a Christian say and why?	What would a non-believer say and why?	What would you say and why?
All people are equal			
All types of discrimination are wrong			
Christians should always be prepared to fight for equality			
Everyone is prejudiced and there is nothing anyone can do to change this			
All Christians should worship together			

Welcome to the Grade Studio

Grade Studio is here to help you improve your grades by working through typical questions you might find on an examination paper. For a full explanation of how this feature works and how exam questions are structured, see page 14. For a full explanation of Assessment Objectives and Levels of Response, see pages x–xi in the Introduction.

AO1

Question

Explain Christian teaching about whether men and women are equal.　　　　　　**[6 marks]**

Student's answer

Christians believe that God created men and women equal. It says in the Bible, 'male and female created he them'. Therefore they must be equal and should be able to do the same things. Some Christians might also believe the story in the second creation account in Genesis, which says that Eve was made from Adam's rib. This may mean that women are inferior to men. The Bible seems to accept that women are not equal because St Paul said they are not allowed to speak in church. Their role is to be a wife and mother like Mary the Mother of Jesus.

Examiner's comment

The candidate has given a satisfactory answer to the question. There are two relevant points but neither is explained in any detail. In order to reach Level 3 the candidate needs to give more information and examples. The candidate could also use more technical terms from the specification to show the breadth of their knowledge and understanding.

Student's improved answer

Christians believe that God created men and women equal. It says in the Bible, 'male and female created he them'. Therefore they must be equal. Some Christians might also believe the story in the second creation account in Genesis, which says that Eve was made from Adam's rib. This may mean that women are inferior to men. The Bible seems to accept that women are not equal because St Paul said they are not allowed to speak in church. Their role is to be a wife and mother like Mary the Mother of Jesus.

Although in the past many people might have shared this view of women as being secondary to men, Christian views have changed over the last hundred years. Today most Christians would say that God made all people equal and that this includes men and women. Women now have the same rights as men and, in recent years, women have been able to become priests or ministers in many denominations of the Christian church. Therefore, women should be seen and treated as equal to men in society and everywhere else. The Roman Catholic church sees women and men as having different roles but as being equally important.

Examiner's comment

This is now a good answer to the question. The candidate has shown a sufficiently clear understanding of the question. There is good description and explanation of a variety of different attitudes to equality. The information is presented clearly and there is good use of technical terms.

AO2

Question

'Men and women are not equal.' Discuss this statement. You should include different, supported points of view and a personal viewpoint. You must refer to Christianity in your answer. **[12 marks]**

Student's answer

Christians might say that, if God intended men and women equal, then he would have made them the same. But they are different and so they can't be equal. Some Christians might also say that God created women to be helpmates to men, and that they are made weaker because they don't have to work but have to give birth to babies and stay at home, while men have to work.

Examiner's comment

The candidate has given a limited answer to the question. There are two points but they both address the same issue and neither is expanded very far. In order to to reach Level 4 the candidate needs to give alternative viewpoints and also include a personal response.

Student's improved answer

Christians might say that, if God intended men and women equal, then he would have made them the same. But they are different and so they can't be equal. Some Christians might also say that God created women to be helpmates to men, and that they are made weaker because they don't have to work but just have to give birth to babies and stay at home, while men have to work.

Examiner's comment

This is now a good answer to the question. The candidate has shown a clear understanding of the question and has presented a range of views supported by evidence and argument. The answer explains Christian views, amongst others, and includes a personal viewpoint, which is also supported.

The majority of Christians and other people would disagree with this statement. Though it might appear from the Bible that women are inferior to men, many people would say that this simply reflects the time in which it was written. God created both sexes and every one is equal before God. Some Christians would show how Jesus treated women as equals by speaking to them or mixing with them, which was unusual in his time. Others might say that if Jesus thought they were equal he would have had both men and women disciples. This is why some Christians such as Roman Catholics believe that men and women have very different roles to perform in life and in Christian worship. This does not mean they don't see them as equal, just different. My personal opinion is that it is obvious that men and women are equal.

You can see that they are equal just by looking at how they work and what they do. Nowadays both sexes are able to do the same things and there is no difference. If any religion teaches that they are not equal, then I believe that the religion is wrong.

These specimen answers provide an outline of how you could construct your response. Space does not allow us to give a full response. The examiner will be looking for more detail in your actual exam responses.

Exam**Café**

Welcome to Exam Café

Now you have finished the course/Topic, it is time to revise and prepare for the examination. The key to success in any exam is the revision and preparation leading up to it. The key to good revision is to 'work smart'. This section will guide you in knowing what is needed for success and, just as important, what is not. So don't panic! Think positive because the examiner will. GCSE is about what you *can* do, not what you can't.

Key points to note at this stage

1 Your revision will need to focus on what the examiner is looking for in the answers so that you can achieve the best possible mark. Remember that the examiners are looking for the AO1 and AO2 assessment objectives. Each of these objectives is worth 50 per cent of the total mark.

2 You also need to know that the exam questions on the paper are designed to test your performance with both AO1 and AO2 objectives. Each question will be made up of five parts:

- Four AO1 parts, of which three check your knowledge and one tests your understanding and analysis.

- One question testing AO2 – your ability to consider different points of view on a particular issue and how much you can express your own points of view with relevant evidence and argument.

Once you understand what the examiner is looking for, it will be time to turn to your revision programme.

How to get started

An important key to success with any exam is the preparation beforehand. While few people enjoy the process of revision, it is something that is vital for success. Your class teacher will also discuss revision with you. Below are some suggestions and ideas that can be employed:

1 It is vital to revise in plenty of time before the exam. Do not leave everything to the last minute.

2 Design a revision timetable and be realistic about what can be achieved.

3 Revision is a personal matter and we all learn in different ways. Remember that many revision skills can be transferred between different subjects.

4 These are some suggested revision techniques:

- Create summary cards for each topic – a maximum of 5–10 bullet points on each card.

- Create lists of key words and terms. Ask somebody to test you on them or hang them around the house.

- Create a mind map to summarise a major topic.

- Design cards with a word or idea on one side and a question/ definition or answer on the other. These allow you to be tested by family members or friends who may not have much subject knowledge.

- Create an A–Z list on a certain topic. This involves writing the 26 letters of the alphabet down the side of a page and then having to write a key word or teaching connected to that topic for each letter.

- Remember that religious teachings do not have to be learned word-for-word. It is acceptable to paraphrase them.

5 Break your revision into sessions of 5–10 minutes to start with (this can be increased as you become much better at it). Give yourself a short break (of about 5 minutes) and then go back to revising. Remember that spending time revising when nothing is going in is as bad as doing no revision at all.

6 Try answering questions on past papers then marking them with the mark scheme yourself. Alternatively, you can write your own questions and develop your own mark scheme. Answer the questions and use the levels of response to mark them.

7 Finally, remember that if you go into revision with a negative attitude you are ultimately going to make it much tougher on yourself.

ExamCafé

Revision
Common errors and mistakes

So the day of the exam has arrived. Remember that you are not the first to sit exams and you will not be the last. However, learn from the experience of others and do not fall into any of the following exam traps:

Misreading the question:
Take a minute and read the question carefully. Surprisingly, a large number of candidates do not read the questions properly. They simply see a word and feel they have to start writing. No matter how good your answer is, if it does not answer the question it will not gain you any marks.

Wasting valuable time: The exam is a race against the clock. Match the length of your response to the number of marks being awarded. A one-mark question can be answered with a single word or a sentence and not a paragraph.

Disorganised waffle: Written answers, especially AO2 style answers, require you to plan your answer carefully. It requires a range of viewpoints including religious responses and your own views. Be careful and do not let your own views take over.

Poor selection of knowledge: Choose good examples that help you to develop and explain your ideas.

It is Religious Studies after all: Remember that the subject is Religious Studies and you will be tested on your knowledge and understanding of religion and its impact on the lives of individuals and communities. Make sure your answers contain relevant religious ideas.

Know the exam paper: Make sure that you fully understand the layout and instructions for the exam paper. In particular, focus on which questions you must do and how many questions you are required to do.

Revision checklist

The details of the course are known as the Specification. It is broken down into the Topics listed below. There is a summary of the key areas within each Topic that you need to know about.

TOPIC 1 RELIGION AND HUMAN RELATIONSHIPS

For this Topic you must:
- know the meaning of the technical terms in the specification so that you can answer factual questions such as 'What is meant by contraception?'
- know and understand the roles of men and women in a Christian family and in the Church family
- know and understand how marriage ceremonies reflect Christian teaching and also be able to explain attitudes towards civil partnerships
- be able to explain different Christian attitudes towards divorce, re-marriage after divorce and contraception.

TOPIC 2 RELIGION AND MEDICAL ETHICS

For this Topic you must:
- know and understand Christian teachings about the sanctity of life and how this belief is reflected in the issues in this Topic
- be able to explain different Christian attitudes towards issues of abortion, fertility treatment, cloning, euthanasia, suicide, and the use of animals in medical research.

TOPIC 3 RELIGION, POVERTY AND WEALTH

For this Topic you must:
- focus on Christian understandings of the causes of hunger, poverty and disease
- be able to explain Christian responses to these issues, including giving money to charity as well as practical responses
- know Christian teachings about the use of money and ways in which it should not be used, for example gambling or lending at interest
- be able to explain what is meant by 'moral' and 'immoral' and what Christians might consider moral and immoral occupations.

TOPIC 4 RESPONSIBILITY FOR THE PLANET

For this Topic you must:
- be able to outline a scientific view of the origin of the world, for example the 'Big Bang' theory, and show an understanding of the theory of evolution through natural selection
- know the meaning of the terms 'creation', 'evolution', 'Big Bang' and 'natural selection'
- be able to outline the creation stories from Genesis and the different ways Christians understand them
- have a knowledge of Christian teachings that can be used to develop views about the relationship between animals and people, and how they should be treated
- understand the concept of stewardship and how this affects Christian attitudes to the use of the world and its resources, and to environmental issues.

TOPIC 5 WAR, PEACE AND HUMAN RIGHTS

For this Topic you must:
- be able to give a detailed explanation of the Just War theory and Christian attitudes towards war
- explain Christian approaches to the use of violence and different attitudes towards pacifism
- be aware of the Universal Declaration of Human Rights and know at least six examples of Human Rights
- show an understanding of the Christian teachings that could be used to support Human Rights.

TOPIC 6 PREJUDICE AND EQUALITY

For this Topic you must:
- be able to explain Christians teachings about equality
- be able to explain Christian attitudes towards racism and gender issues, especially concerning the role of women in Christian society
- show understanding of Christian attitudes towards other religions, including beliefs about spreading the teachings of Christianity and conversion
- be able to give examples of groups of Christians who work and worship together
- know the meaning of the terms 'missionary work', 'evangelism' and 'ecumenism'.

ExamCafé

Exam preparation

Sample student answer

Now you have done some serious revision it is time to see what sort of response to the questions will get good marks in the exam. Here are some examples of responses with comments from the examiner to show you what is good about them and how they could be improved.

Remember examiners will use levels of response for part d, which is AO1, and part e, which is AO2. For parts a, b and c, responses will be point marked. This means that if there is one mark allocated for the question, only one point is expected, if two marks are allocated, then two points are expected and so on. Part a is worth one mark, b two marks and c three marks.

AO1 a-c

Here are some AO1 point-marked questions and example responses from Topic 1: Religion and human relationships.

> **What is a divorce?** (1 mark)
>
> Ending a marriage.

'What is?' just means describe something – in this case, divorce.

Examiner says
Correct.

> **Give two religious aspects of a Christian marriage service.** (2 marks)
>
> The ring, the vows and the confetti.

Check that you write about 'religious' aspects.

Examiner says
Responses 1 and 2 are correct, but response 3 is not a religious aspect.

> **Why might Roman Catholics not want to be divorced?** (3 marks)
>
> It breaks their vows. Marriage is a sacrament with promises made to God which cannot be broken. They will probably not be able to be remarried in church.

Here, although there is only one mark per point, you will need to be precise and concise in your response.

Examiner says
Three good reasons given.

AO1 Part d questions

Some AO1 answers are marked by levels of response. These are the part d of the questions and are worth six marks each. However, just because they are worth six marks it does not mean that examiners want to see six short points or three developed points in the answer. Instead the examiner is looking for a level of understanding. The higher the level, then the higher the level of understanding required. This could be done by referring to several points and expanding each a little or by developing one or two points in greater detail. Below is a sample answer.

> **Explain how Christians might respond to someone who wants to commit suicide.**
> **(6 marks)**

When answering this question, ask yourself the question 'Why?' as soon as you have written down a reason. There are different levels of explanation, and the examiner is looking for depth, not for a superficial level.

Response 1

Christians might say that it is wrong to commit suicide because it is killing, which is against the Ten Commandments. They might say that only God has the right to take life. They might try to cheer the person up by talking to them.

Examiner says
This is a satisfactory response, reaching Level 2. The information given is relevant, and accurate reasons have been chosen. However, the response is not well developed and is essentially one-sided, giving only one explanation.

Response 2

Christians might say that it is wrong to commit suicide because it is murder, which is against the Ten Commandments. They might say that only God has the right to give life and to take it away.

Some Christians might try to talk the person out of it by showing them how much God loves them.

They may also persuade them to speak to an organisation like the Samaritans who help people in these situations. Also, they might show people how much they are loved and that there are still good things in life.

Examiner says
This is a good response. It contains much of the satisfactory response but it is much more developed. The reasons for different views are explained. This response would reach Level 3.

Exam Café

Exam preparation

Sample student answer

AO2

Part e of each question in the exam will be an AO2 question asking you to explain different points of view about a particular issue. It also gives you an opportunity to present your own personal viewpoint. However, please remember that all viewpoints on a particular issue must be backed up with good evidence, argument and reasoning. Part e of each question is worth 12 marks, or 50 per cent of the total, so it is important to think carefully about how you are going to tackle these questions.

Planning an AO2 answer

These questions want different points of view about a particular issue. Your answer could therefore be structured in the following way:

Paragraph 1: Explain a view that will *agree* with the statement in the question. Offer evidence, beliefs and teachings to back up the point of view.

Paragraph 2: Explain a *different* view from what the statement is suggesting. Again you need to offer evidence, beliefs and teachings to back up your point of view.

Paragraph 3: Include your own personal viewpoint about the issue raised. Again you need to offer evidence, beliefs and arguments to support your point of view. The examiner does not mind which point of view you take, there is no right or wrong answer. Instead the examiner is interested in your ability to reason and argue. If you really do not have a strong point of view on this issue just go for the viewpoint that you can best argue.

Here is an AO2 question and some example responses from Topic 6: Prejudice and equality.

'Christians should try to convert everyone to their religion.' (12 marks)

Response 1

Christians believe that it is their duty to make everyone join their religion so that they can go to heaven. Some people might say that this is wrong and people should be left to decide their religion for themselves.

Response 2

Christians believe that it is their duty to make everyone join their religion so that they can go to heaven. This is because Christianity is a proselytising religion and the 'gospels' are the 'good news' that they have to spread.

Some people might say that this is wrong and people should be left to decide their religion for themselves. It is wrong to try to persuade someone to join your religion just because you believe in it.

Examiner says

This is Level 1. Two relevant viewpoints are stated but there is little support to back them up. This is a simplistic response and shows limited understanding of the question. There is no use of technical terms.

Examiner says

This is Level 2. This is a better answer as it explains to the examiner what the candidate understands the question to be about. However, although two viewpoints are stated and slightly developed, the response is still rather limited.

Response 3

Christians believe that it is part of their duty as followers of Jesus to make everyone join their religion so that they can go to heaven. This is because Christianity is a proselytising religion and the 'gospels' are the 'good news' that they have to spread. Jesus commanded them to go into the world to preach the gospel. They also believe that becoming a Christian is the only way in which people can reach heaven and the presence of God.

Some people might say that this is wrong and people should be left to decide their religion for themselves. It is wrong to try to persuade someone to join your religion just because you believe in it. Religion is personal thing and no one should try to force you into it.

Others may think that everyone can listen to whatever they like and can then make their own decisions. It is no different to advertising anything else. My personal opinion is that it is very difficult for Christians not to try to persuade people to join their religion.

Response 4

Christians believe that it is part of their duty as followers of Jesus to make everyone join their religion so that they can go to heaven. This is because Christianity is a proselytising religion and the 'gospels' are the 'good news' that they have to spread. Jesus commanded them to go into the world to preach the gospel. They also believe that becoming a Christian is the only way in which people can reach heaven and the presence of God.

Some people might say that this is wrong and people should be left to decide their religion for themselves. It is wrong to try to persuade someone to join your religion just because you believe in it. Religion is a personal thing and no one should try to force you into it.

Others may think that everyone can listen to whatever they like and can then make their own decisions. It is no different to advertising anything else and it is up to people to decide whether to respond or not.

Christians believe it is part of their religious duty to convert people. Jesus preached the good news and they have to do the same. However, I do not like people knocking on my door trying to persuade me to join their faith and I think it should be left to individuals to come to their own decisions.

ExamCafé

Exam preparation
Understanding exam language

Examiners try to keep questions short and clear. To do this they use special trigger words to hint at how you should respond to the questions. Below is a list of common trigger words. You should familiarise yourself with these words:

State	Usually used in AO1 questions worth 1–3 marks. This means 'write down a fact about something', for example *State the Just War theory*.
Give	This is used instead of 'state' and requires the same sort of response.
List	This is used instead of 'give' or 'state' and requires the same sort of response.
Describe	This is used in AO1 questions and means 'tell the examiner factual information about the item or idea'. An example is *Describe the Big Bang theory*, which means 'write down factual information about the Big Bang theory'.
Give an account of	This is asking for the same sort of response as 'describe', for example *Give an account Christian teachings about the sanctity of life*.
Explain	This means 'show that you understand something', for example *Explain different Christian attitudes towards issues of abortion*. An 'explain' response will include some knowledge, but the best responses will give a range of ideas and reasons.
Why	This word is used as shorthand for 'explain'. Put the word 'explain' in front of it and you will know what to do, for example *Why are there different Christian attitudes towards issues of abortion?* is the same as *Explain why there are different Christian attitudes towards issues of abortion*.
How	This can be used to ask you for factual information, for example *How do marriage ceremonies reflect Christian teaching?* It can also be used for questions that are asking for understanding where there is a mixture of fact and understanding required.
Important	This word is used frequently in AO1 part d questions and it indicates that you need to say why Christians should or should not do/believe something. An example is *Explain why the Genesis creation stories are important to Christians*, which means, *Give reasons to explain why the Genesis creation stories are thought of as special in Christianity*.

Examiner Tips
Planning and structuring an answer

In the Grade Studios you have been shown how to build levels of response. This is really important for the AO1 responses to part d worth six marks and the AO2 responses to part e worth 12 marks. In each case follow this structure:

- Check you really know what the question is asking. In the AO2 questions work out the key word or words in the statement, for example *If science is right about the origins of the world, religion must be wrong. Discuss this statement*. The key words here are 'right' and 'wrong'. If the answer does not deal with them, then it will be awarded a low mark.
- Make a note of key points to include all AO1 responses and use a diagram to note down viewpoints for AO2.
- Begin your answer with a brief mention of what the question is asking you to do.
- Write clearly and concisely. DON'T WAFFLE.
- Reach a conclusion at the end of your answer. In the case of an AO1 answer this could be a brief summary sentence, for example *So for these reasons Christians might want to take care of the environment*. In the case of an AO2 answer the conclusion should include a **personal view** (with supporting reasons/argument) and a **brief summing up** of the different views you have expressed.
- Leave a gap of a few lines between each answer. This is in case you wish to add further ideas/information later (if you don't, there is no need to worry).
- If you have any time left at the end of your exam use it constructively. Check your answer makes sense. Check your answer is responding to the question set. Check your use of English, grammar and spelling. Check you have answered the required number of questions. **Remember when you hand in your answer paper at the end of the exam it is probably the last time you will ever see it. Make sure it is your best possible effort.**

Glossary

Abortion: deliberate termination of pregnancy by removal and destruction of the foetus.

Adultery: a married person having a sexual relationship with someone to whom they are not married.

Annulment: a marriage terminated by the Church because it was not valid.

Atomic weapon: a device which uses a nuclear explosion as a weapon.

Big Bang theory: the scientific theory that the universe came into being as a result of a cosmic explosion.

Charity: to give help or money to those in need.

Civil partnership: legal recognition of a same-sex relationship with a registry office ceremony.

Clone: an individual organism or cell produced asexually from one ancestor to which they are genetically identical.

Commitment: a bond between a couple.

Compassion: sympathy and concern for others.

Conscientious objector: someone who refuses to fight in a war on the basis of their conscience.

Creationists: Christians who believe that the creation of the universe happened in exactly the way Genesis describes it.

Crusade: religiously sanctioned war, often about the control of a sacred place.

Darwinism: the theory Charles Darwin put forward for evolution.

Discrimination: unjust or prejudicial treatment because of race, age, gender or disability.

Divorce: the legal ending of a marriage.

Ecumenical: different Christian denominations working together.

Embryo: a foetus before it is 4 months old.

Environmental issues: a concern for the way humans exploit natural resources.

Equality: treating people as equals regardless of gender, race or religious beliefs.

Euthanasia: when someone is helped to die without pain before they would have died naturally.

Evangelism: persuading others to share your faith.

Evolution: the way in which animals and plants adapt to their surroundings – the survival of the fittest.

Fertility treatment: medical treatment to help a woman become pregnant.

Genetic engineering: the deliberate modification of the characteristics of an organism by manipulating its genetic material.

Immoral: not conforming to accepted standards of behaviour.

Intelligent Design theory: the idea that the complexity of life on earth and the fact that conditions on earth are just right for life prove that it must have had a designer.

Just War theory: the belief that wars can be morally justified if they follow certain criteria.

Justice: fairness in society and the world.

LEDC: less economically developed country.

MEDC: more economically developed country.

Medical ethics: questions of morality that are raised by medical situations.

Moral: conforming to accepted standards of behaviour.

Natural selection: the way animals and plants adapt to life or die out.

New Testament: collection of 27 books forming the second section of the Christian Bible.

Nuclear pacifism: belief that the use of a nuclear weapon can never be justified.

Old Testament: that part of the Christian Bible which the Christian Church shares with Judaism, comprising 39 books covering the Hebrew Canon, and in the case of certain denominations, some books of the Apocrypha.

Pacifism: the belief that fighting, violence and war can never be justified.

Philanthropist: someone who donates money, goods, services or time to help a cause which benefits society.

Pollution: destruction of the natural world by human activity.

Prejudice: making judgements not based on reason or actual experience.

Pre-marital sex: having a sexual relationship before marriage.

Promiscuity: having many sexual partners without commitment.

Proselytising: trying to convert people from their religion to yours.

Quaker: a member of the Christian denomination also known as the Religious Society of Friends.

Racism: prejudice, discrimination or ill treatment against someone because of their race.

Re-marriage: marrying again after divorce. Also after annulment or widowhood.

Sacrament: a special action which brings Christians closer to God.

Sacred/sanctity: holy, having something of God or the divine.

Sanctity of life: the belief that all life is given by God and is therefore sacred.

Sexism: prejudice, stereotyping or discrimination, typically against women, on the basis of sex.

Sin: an act which goes against God's will.

Stewardship: the belief that humans are caretakers of the planet for God.

Suicide: deliberately ending one's own life.

Tithe: the Christian practice of giving a tenth of their income to charity.

Trade restrictions: restrictions made by one country about the amounts and types of goods it will allow into the country from other countries.

Violence: the use of physical force, with the intention to harm.

Vows: sacred promises a couple make at their marriage.

Index